TWISTS TURNS & TRUTHS

Linda —
here's to purpose -
and our continuing
collaboration !
Love, Jayne

Praise for
TWISTS TURNS & TRUTHS

"There is nothing more important than finding and living your life purpose. Master Hand Analyst Jayne Sanders has found hers and reading about her heart-warming, roller coaster journey will no doubt inspire you to find and live your own."

Richard Unger
Founder & Director, International
Institute of Hand Analysis

"I felt like I was having a conversation with my closest friend. Jayne has written a wise, vulnerable, deeply meaningful book."

Rachael Jayne Groover
Best-selling author of *Powerful and Feminine*
and Creator of Art of Feminine Presence

"The phrases, "it's right at your fingertips" and "it's all in your hands" are brought to bear in this timely and engaging book. Jayne's personal stories take you on a vivid journey all while weaving in the scientific wisdom that is literally imprinted on our hands. I have experienced and benefited from her expertise firsthand. Jayne's work provides an accessible map we can turn to for a deeper understanding when needed. A must read for anyone seeking to understand oneself at an even deeper level."

Dana Busch, PsyD, MPH, MA
Clinical Health Psychologist

"If you ever wished you had an instruction manual for your life, you need to read this book! Jayne opens the door to what else is possible for you and your life through her engaging stories and fascinating wisdom woven throughout her book. I couldn't stop reading it once I started!"

Tami Gulland
Founder of Energetic IQ™ Mastery

"Having personally benefitted greatly from her expertise, I can truly say that Jayne Sanders is a master at what she does. Through the stories of her book, Jayne shares her wit, wisdom and love for personal transformation as she guides readers in beginning to answer life's most important question, 'What is the purpose of my life?'."

Chris Natzke
Black Belt Leadership Speaking & Coaching

"As a client of Jayne's, I've experienced first-hand how this work can give you valuable insight into your own successes and challenges; the process makes sense of your gifts and gives you the tools to move forward in a purposeful way. Her willingness to open up in an authentic way and share how her experiences and complexities are reflected in her own hands gave me even more insight into the process. I believe any reader will be able to relate to her stories, gain a little more knowledge into what hand analysis is, and want to dive into finding their own Master and Student paths. It truly is an eye-opener."

Catherine Tidd
Author of *Confessions of a Mediocre Widow*

"Jayne teaches through the emotional stories of her life, in this hard-to-put-down book. I felt like I was having a conversation with a friend. And I'll never look at my hands passively again."

Rick Arthur
CFO

"A truly inspirational, authentic and charismatic read! I was captivated throughout the entire book and Jayne emulates so many powerful stories that bring joy and happiness."

Mollie Savage
Wealth Management Advisor

"This book makes it impossible not to know Jayne and feel like a friend of hers. Her descriptions of her ups and downs and characteristics involved allowed me to look more closely at my life and increase my awareness. What could be better than that? Awareness and growth are essential these days..."

Bob Dodge
Trusted Advisor, The Alternative Board – Denver West

"Having experienced Jayne's profound and life-changing work, it was even more fascinating to read her stories and how they show up in her hands. I truly enjoyed reading about her experiences, which were told with her authentic and entertaining voice. Jayne draws the readers into the emotions of her stories and then shares valuable information they can apply to their own lives. Read this book – I didn't want it to end!"

Michelle L. Wilson, MA, LPC
The Breakthrough Mentor for Entrepreneurs and Leaders

"*Twists Turns and Truths: The Life and Lines of a Master Scientific Hand Analyst* by Jayne Sanders is a thought-provoking read with an inspiring voice, scientific hand analysis, and personal stories.

Each chapter is written with genuine honesty and an admirable openness, revealing different experiences which she then uses to show how these are seen in her hands. Several examples of hand analysis follow each chapter which makes it easy to understand and learn the significance of moments in your life through details in your hands. Also throughout are lovely poems which tie into various stories. The poems have a stunning lyrical style with profound emotion and depth drawn out of each, making them perfectly fitted to the voice and tone of the memoir aspects. *Twists Turns and Truths* is a unique read with honest stories told through an emotional lens and with a focus on scientific hand analysis, ideal for those seeking honest memoirs, genuine voices, and unique topics."

Liz Konkel
Readers' Favorite Professional Book Reviewers

"*Twists Turns & Truths* is a nonfiction memoir written by Jayne Sanders. The author has been involved in and fascinated by Scientific Hand Analysis ever since she was first exposed to it in 2012. In this memoir, she demystifies SHA and shows how it is NOT what many consider to be a carnival act that predicts the future. As she became more familiar with SHA, she was able to use that knowledge to understand her life choices and issues and to learn how to best use her strengths, gifts, and skills.

When I began reading Jayne Sanders' memoir, I was intrigued by the concept of hand analysis but had never really given it any thought or credence. I found her introduction to contain a well-written and knowledgeable account of what Scientific Hand Analysis is -- and isn't. Armed with my new insights, I set off on a most enjoyable journey with the author. Sanders' horse stories are wonderful. I loved getting to know each of her equine soul mates; the stories of their time together and the depth of their relationships taught me so much about that bond between horse and man.

While writing an engaging and honest memoir, Sanders shares what she's learned about her own traits through Scientific Hand Analysis and how they've played out in her life story. At the end of each chapter, she shows the reader how to identify the markings described in that chapter, which I found both fascinating and illuminating. *Twists Turns & Truths* is an enlightening, well-written and enjoyable memoir which is also an impressive and knowledgeable introduction to SHA that made me want to learn more about it. *Twists Turns & Truths: The Life and Lines of a Master Scientific Hand Analyst* is most highly recommended."

Jack Magnus
Readers' Favorite Professional Book Reviewers

TWISTS
TURNS
&TRUTHS

A Memoir

The Life and Lines of a
Master Scientific Hand Analyst

JAYNE SANDERS

FULL GALLOP PRESS

Published by Full Gallop Press

ISBN: 978-0-9723810-9-3

Publisher's Cataloging-in-Publication data

Names: Sanders, Jayne. author.
Title: Twists turns and truths : the life and lines of a master scientific
    hand analyst / Jayne Sanders.
Description: Lakewood [Colorado] : Full Gallop Press, 2019. Paperback.
    Also being published as an ebook.
Identifiers: ISBN: 978-0-9723810-1-7
Subjects: LCSH: Autobiography. | Palmistry.
BISAC: BIOGRAPHY & AUTOBIOGRAPHY / Personal Memoirs
Classification: LCC BF940.S | DDC 920 SANDERS–dc22

Printed in the United States of America.

Book cover and page design by Michelle M. White

To Beau, Comet, Darby, Bo, LT, Duke, and Breeze—
the equine teachers and loves of my life.
Darby is still with me and could possibly outlive me.
Now there's a quandary.

TABLE OF CONTENTS

INTRODUCTION

I promise not to chicken out on you.

To start, let me say that I was blown away. The very first Scientific Hand Analysis I received in 2012 answered questions I didn't even know I had. It explained so much about my life, the ups and downs, the wins and losses, the joys and pains. It also answered big questions I *did* know I had, gave me deep insight, opened me up to innate gifts I hadn't recognized, and provided my North Star for purpose, fulfillment, and taking action on problem areas. It changed my life.

Oh how I wish I found this earlier in life! Now I'm doing everything I can to spread the word, to bring this amazing modality out into the open so more people can experience it and the guidance and confidence it delivers.

So I want to share some of these discoveries with you, told through my memoir of sorts—selected stories of my life that demonstrate many of the traits that are etched in the blueprint in my hands.

My hope is that you will laugh, wince, cry, and cheer with me as you read these stories. It is actually quite scary, vulnerable, to share some of these tales. But I don't want to hold back, because I know that readers are too smart for that. I know you will see right through me, that you will recognize when I am chickening out and glossing over or leaving out the difficult or potentially embarrassing or controversial stuff. I want to be brave.

Some stories are about horses I have loved, but most involve humans. I have changed the names of people involved, but not the horses, as I know they don't mind.

What I've discovered through my own story and those of my clients is that your hands will tell you about you and your life. They will answer the big questions many people ask—Who am I at my core? Why am I here on the planet? What legacy am I meant to leave? What are my innate gifts and talents? Why do those challenging patterns keep showing up? What can I do to reduce pain and trouble in my life? Why do I feel lost, confused, bored, overwhelmed, or depressed? Why am I experiencing relationship, money, or health issues? How can I adjust, and what steps can I take to make life even better?

My desire with this book is to demonstrate to you the depth and accuracy of Scientific Hand Analysis, using stories from my life and guiding you to apply relevant markings to your life. I want to share how the characteristics I have and have had, show up in my hands. Your hands will tell much of your story too.

My hope is that you will see some similar strengths and challenges in your own life, and if you are interested, learn how to take action to use the strengths for good, and reduce the more troublesome events and feelings.

I'd still be writing if I included every story from my life of any meaning. And I'd also still be writing if I addressed all the markings I have in my hands that are relevant to each story. So I've selected merely a few of the more prominent and important markings and described the topline of each. My intention is not to provide a primer, or a Scientific Hand Analysis (SHA) 101 how-to book. My intentions are to help some of you understand yourselves and your life better, spread the word about this life-changing work, so accurate that forbes.com wrote an article about it, and instill in you the fascination about SHA that most people experience when they hear about it.

I have referred to some of my markings several times intentionally, so that you can see how the same marking can show up differently in your life, as they do in mine. The more important markings have several messages for us.

I want to trigger some curiosity about what your hands have to tell you and help you identify a bit of what is there. And, I hope some of you can learn from the mistakes I share in my stories, perhaps recognizing some of the markings in your own hands and increasing your awareness of how related challenges may show up in your lives so you can take action.

This work is what guided me to living on purpose, *finally*. SHA profoundly changed me and my life, in the best way. I started studying it and haven't stopped, with the first five years devoted to earning every certification possible. I am now at Level IV, the highest, indicating I am certified to teach Scientific Hand Analysis, and I earned the title Master a few years ago once I surpassed one thousand clients.

It is not predictive nor fortune-telling. I can't tell someone when they will meet their soul mate nor how many children they will have. Nor do I want to. Here is what I know for certain—regardless of how good your life is now, if you take action on the information in your hands, it will only get better. That is the only "prediction" I make.

So please join me as I take you on a journey through some of the ins and outs, up and downs, struggles and accomplishments, heart wins and heartbreaks of my life— and how they show up in my hands.

THE BASICS OF SCIENTIFIC HAND ANALYSIS

The lines in your hands mimic the neural pathways in your brain. These lines can change, disappear, grow additions, and new lines can form as well. The fingerprints are formed in utero at fourteen to sixteen weeks but never change, otherwise, the FBI would be in deep doo-doo, right? Fingerprints can even appear in the palms, as they do in well over half of my clients' hands. So those people have fingerprints inside their palm prints. Scientific hand analysts get information about you from the fingerprints and the lines, also from the shape of your hands, how your fingers are set on the palm, how they relate to each other . . . everything.

Fingerprints will never change, but everything else in your hands, the lines, shape, and more, certainly can. As life experiences and events change the neural pathways in your brain, these changes can show up in your hands. The major lines won't make a U-turn, but new, little lines can form, other lines can break, and still others can create geometric shapes within the palm such as squares, circles, and diamonds.

Richard Unger developed this database over a forty-year period, analyzing more than 30,000 hands. A neurosurgeon at Stanford wrote the foreword to Richard's book, *LifePrints*. Also, forbes.com wrote about the accuracy of this work. One of the aspects I love about SHA is that the results are independent of how you interpret questions on an assessment, the mood you're in, what 'score' you want. The information is etched into your hands.

A few general rules: The longer the line or the bigger the area, the more time and energy you spend in whatever that line or area represents. The shorter the line, the less time and energy. The more curve in the line, the more emotion you access or use in whatever that line represents. For example, a curved head line—usually the middle of three major lines in the hand and running primarily horizontally, the line that provides indications of how you think, make decisions, prefer information presented to you, and more—would indicate you use emotion along with logic in your decisions and how you think.

Every marking in the hands has both a *Master path* and *Student path*. Master path feels good. The more Master paths you're on, the easier it is to live in alignment with your innate purpose. And living on purpose is the only way to the deeper and more consistent joy and fulfillment that everyone desires.

Student paths are all the yucky feelings in life—feeling stuck, confused, lost, overwhelmed, bored, frustrated, burnt out, angry, depressed, procrastinating, relationship issues, money trouble. The more Student paths you're on, the more difficult it is to live in alignment with your purpose.

Here's the kicker—no one can be on the Master path of any marking one hundred percent of the time. We are human after all, works in progress. I see myself on Student paths, at least one, every day. The idea is to recognize it and do your best to move to the Master path. Many of the stories in this book exist due to me being on Student paths, at least at that time. And many demonstrate the possible outcomes of Master path living as well.

Gift markings are indications of extra potential talent in different areas. They are very important for several reasons. First, far more than half of all humans on the planet do not have a gift marking. This does not mean that some of them aren't amazing people making a big difference, but if you have a gift marking it's a big deal. If you have multiple gift markings, it's a bigger deal.

Second, gift markings explain the 'how,' the gifts you have to help you fulfill your purpose and make the difference you are meant to make in the world. And third, they're important because they have Student paths as well. Gift marking Student paths are boogers, they can give you a good kick in the tush to get your attention and motivate you to use your gifts. I like to call them wake-up calls, and they can range from tiny pokes to cosmic two-by-fours.

I'm telling you stories of my life so that I can demonstrate how aspects of me and my experiences show up in my hands. These stories reveal my character, my challenges, my mistakes (or growth opportunities, steps through Student paths), and my wins. They give hints as to who I was, who I am now, and who I am becoming.

Even after nearly seven years (as of this writing) and analyzing over 5,000 hands, this work still fascinates me with its accuracy and depth. Keep in mind the markings I reference are merely a teensy few of many in my hands, and their descriptions within are topline only but enough to communicate their key meanings.

At the end of most chapters, I ask that you check your hands (done best in good light with a magnifying glass, preferably a lighted one) to see if you have any of the markings I have described. Doing so will increase your self-awareness, validate some of your strengths and gifts, and explain for you some of the challenges you have faced or are facing in your life.

For those of you who may have concerns how Scientific Hand Analysis fits with religion—my belief is that God tries many ways to help us make the difference we are meant to make in the world. God created us, so that includes the lines and fingerprints in our hands as well. He has given us a blueprint to follow.

Here's what I know—the easiest and most joyful way through life is by following the blueprint in your hands.

CHAPTER 1

MY BIG RED BOY

*My knees buckled as I dropped
to the ground, incredulous. I was
looking at an empty stall. Hay
was strewn out its gate and up
the dirt driveway to the road.*

In my first career, I was transferred to Los
Angeles, and eventually found my way to a ranch in Malibu
that had about thirty horses used for public rides. During
my first ride there, I told Tanya, the proprietor, I wanted to
learn more about horses. It bothered me that every lesson I
took, anywhere, I would arrive to a tacked-up horse, get on,
ride, get off, and leave. I wanted to work with them, understand them, and enjoy the full experience. Tanya told me
she needed volunteers on weekends, and if I helped out,
she would teach me everything I wanted to know. Jackpot.

From that day forward I spent every weekend I possibly could at that ranch until it folded about ten years later. By the end of the first summer, I was taking rides out myself as one of the head wranglers. I got to know every one of those thirty horses, their personalities, gaits, quirks, and which ones to use on which rides with which riders. I was in heaven. My childhood dream to have my own horse kept growing, but I certainly had the next best thing, and in many people's view, even better than the next best thing. I got to ride as much as my seat-bones could handle, with no boarding fees, vet bills, or shoeing costs.

I learned an enormous amount about horses from Tanya, and still feel deep gratitude to her for that life-changing education. She taught me about personalities, gaits, temperaments, riding skills, health treatments, maintenance, and upkeep—impossible to capture it all here.

Horses became a huge part of my life, as did the deep friendships I made with the all-women volunteers and regular riders. Several of these women are still wonderful friends to this day, nearly twenty years later. Sadly, Tanya lost the ranch after a few years when the owner sold the property. To say that period of time was a nightmare is an understatement. All the horses had to be sold. I watched with an extremely heavy heart as my four-legged, gentle, intuitive, healing equine friends were led, sometimes by me, down the long driveway into waiting trailers at the bottom of the hill.

Some of them picked up on their friends' anguish and fear of being separated and mildly resisted. They could have reared, pulled back, become dangerous. But no, they didn't want to hurt anyone, so they slowly and sadly behaved and let themselves be taken away from the life and horses they had known for years. It was absolutely heart-breaking. They were my friends too, and I knew I wouldn't see most of them ever again.

Four of the women regulars bought the horses they rode and moved to a private home across the canyon that had boarding space for five. Another woman who had boarded at Tanya's moved her horse with us. I rode her horse, Beau, often at the ranch, so I was thrilled when Rox-anne moved him to this new facility. She told me I could ride him as much as I wanted, as long as I paid his vet and shoeing bills. Done. And phew, my horsie life was still alive and well after this traumatic upheaval.

I took great care of Beau. He was a fabulous horse. Well, I didn't take good care of him just because he was a fabulous horse, I would have taken care of him anyway. So let's say I *spoiled* him because he was a fabulous horse. He was a tall, muscular red quarter horse with a big, white blaze starting up under his forelock and sliding down over his nose. He was about eighteen years old at the time, a past Western competition blue-ribbon winner in team pen-ning. His left knee, swollen off and on, told that competi-tion story. I was so lucky to be able to ride him. Roxanne told me he had never looked so happy and healthy.

Another friend from the ranch had moved her horse to a different boarding facility. Flossie told me that a few of the owners out there hired an animal communicator to do a session with each of their horses. She said it was amazing and really fun, so I presented the idea to my riding friends at the new barn.

They went for it. Well, three of them did. I scheduled the communicator, and away we went. Jan came out on a

Tuesday and blew our minds. Princess, a big gray Missouri Foxtrotter, was the first horse she talked with. And no, not like you and I talking, it was all silent, telepathy. And everything Jan relayed that Princess said, was definitely something that Princess would say, in the way Princess would say it. I had known that horse and used her in my rides for several years. We were amazed.

I asked Jan, "Horses don't know English, how do they know what you're saying and vice versa?" Jan told me that God, Spirit, Source, a higher power, steps in and translates, and also that animals often communicate by sending pictures telepathically. Okay, I'll go with it, I thought to myself with the accompanying facial expression and shrug.

The next horse she communicated with was Comet, a bossy little Paso Fino who I used at the ranch even more than Princess because he was fun and fast with shockingly smooth gaits. He was always hard to catch, only a couple of us could grab and halter him for our rides in less than five minutes. Comet was a master at letting us get close then dodging us and running just far enough away to be a pain in the butt. He was little in stature but big in personality. And he was goosey, shy around new people, although not spooky out on the trail.

So it certainly surprised us when, as soon as Jan sat in the plastic chair we put inside his stall, he trotted right up to her and put his muzzle on top of her head. "I need to go find her," Jan said he exclaimed to her. "I need to go out into the mountains and find her."

"Who is he talking about?" Jan asked us. My friend Susie and I just looked at each other in amazement and with tears in our eyes. Comet and his daughter Shayna, who were best friends for twelve years, were sold separately. Shayna had been ripped out of his life. He was looking for Shayna. All we could do was cry with him.

Next was Beau, the horse I was riding for Roxanne. I didn't tell Jan I wasn't his owner because I was afraid she might not do the session with him. I adored Beau by then. I wanted to know how he was doing—if he was happy, if he hurt anywhere, and if he was afraid of anything. For that last question, I expected him to say mountain lions as they roamed through our area every once in a while. I already knew he wasn't afraid of rattlesnakes. I would have to make him stop on the trail sometimes to avoid stepping on one or getting bitten. Obviously, he didn't know about poison.

Jan reported this, "He says yes he hurts but he doesn't care because he's never been so happy. The only thing he is afraid of is never seeing you again." I was taken aback. She asked me what his fear was about. I told her I didn't know, that I had no plans of going anywhere. Once again, he told her that he was very worried about never seeing me again. I finally had to fess up and tell Jan I didn't own him, but that the owner was very happy with me and that all was well. But Beau told her that if Roxanne took him from me he would die inside. Huge heart-thunk.

I had no idea he was so attached to me. He was not a physically affectionate horse, as some are. Learning this touched me so deeply, and I was already crying. As soon as Jan started the conversation with him, he laid his big chestnut head on my shoulder, tucked his face under my arm, so lovingly and snuggly. I guess he took Jan's conversation as his chance to get it through my thick skull how much he loved me. I was deeply, profoundly moved. I told him, through Jan, that I adored him and wasn't going anywhere.

That was on a Tuesday. The following Saturday when I arrived at the barn to ride, he was gone. He had known it was going to happen.

I fell to my knees in front of his stall. Hay was strewn out into the aisle. There had obviously been some kind of struggle. Sobbing, I called Jan, thankfully reaching her immediately, and told her Beau was gone. She was nearly as shocked as I was. I asked her if she could do her thing remotely. "Of course," she said and dove in.

My big red boy had been taken just before dawn. He told her he tried to stay away from the two men, but he didn't want to hurt them. Beau was waiting for me to come and save him (insert broken heart). He knew Roxanne was behind it because he heard the men talking about how crazy she was. Beau told Jan he was about ninety minutes away by horse trailer, that it was very pretty where he was but that he didn't care, he was in despair. He told me to keep thinking about him, that he could feel me, to keep looking for him, and that we would find each other again.

Devastation coursed through every cell in my body. Why in the world did Roxanne do this? I called her, many times that day and over the following several days and weeks, but she never answered her phone or returned my calls. Princess' owner, on the spot, offered to loan me the money to buy him. I would have taken her up on it if I could have reached Roxanne, but no go. I had lost my big red boy.

I called every boarding facility I could locate, but there were hundreds in Southern California. I looked for weeks.

I could not find him. After crying myself to sleep for many nights, I finally got into the space of gratitude for the time I had with him. I was so blessed to have had the opportunity to care for and ride such an amazing horse. So instead of crying every night, I evolved to looking at his photo beside my bed (yes, I know how goofy that sounds) and feeling the gratitude.

He had been taken in September. On every ride, after he disappeared, I couldn't help but secretly hope to see him trotting up the trail as we turned a corner in the canyon. Nope. That following December, inexplicably, I started feeling the grief again, crying frequently, wondering how he was doing. I thought what the heck, I might as well call Roxanne again. I almost dropped my phone when she answered the call. "Oh Jayne, I'm so sorry. I know I hurt you terribly. The boarder threatened to lock him in his stall because I owed her money, so I couldn't tell anyone I was leaving. I'm so sorry."

Well, why couldn't you have told me soon afterwards? I asked her silently inside my head.

She continued, "But it's so weird that you're calling me right now, I just decided to sell him. Do you want to buy him?"

Chills ran up and down my spine. It was Beau, reaching out to me, that had triggered this new phase of tears and my call to Roxanne after three months. I asked his price, which was ridiculously high, probably three times what he was worth, and told her I would get back to her. She knew she had me. She knew how much I loved that horse. My attempt at negotiating fell on deaf ears. Roxanne was locked onto her asking price, saying she had another buyer waiting if I didn't want to buy him at that amount. I called Princess' owner who had offered to loan me money three months earlier on the day Beau was taken. I'm sure she was not thinking it would be that much. But the next day, thanks to that friend who personally understood the unparalleled bond between horse and human, I had an envelope full of cash in my hand.

Roxanne insisted I meet her brother way out in the Valley, an hour from Malibu because he conducted her business dealings. She would not tell me where Beau was. I knew she was afraid I would steal him, which is so ridiculous I can hardly even write this sentence. I called one of the local haulers.

"Johnny, I need you to pick up a horse for me. I know this sounds weird, but I don't know where he is yet. I will know around noon. Is there any way this can work?" I knew how silly that sounded.

"Sure darlin,'" he said. He was a cowboy, a good ole boy, and used to work for the Reagans at their California ranch. "I have a job this morning, I'll just pull over and wait to hear from you, no problem." How cool and sweet was that?

Anyway, once I paid Roxanne's brother the money and signed their sales agreement, he told me where Beau was. Yep, a ninety-minute drive by trailer from our barn, on top of a small mountain with gorgeous views, exactly as he had described to Jan the day he was taken. I asked Johnny to call me once he got Beau loaded and was headed back to Malibu. Then on the way home from the valley, I talked out loud in my car to who was now *my* horse. My lifelong dream had come true. "Get in the trailer, Beau. I'm coming to get you. It will be a man with a trailer, a friend, so get in, you're coming home." Tears poured down my face. I was quivering with excitement.

Johnny called an hour later and told me in his thick cowboy accent, "Jayne, it was the weirdest thing. When I pulled up to the corral, your horse was waiting at the gate for me. He kept trying to get in the trailer before I could get the ramp all the way down." Of course, he did. Beau knew he was coming home.

And that's how I got my beloved horse Beau, the equine love of my life. I had him for ten years.

I wrote the poem below within a couple weeks of buying him. I still can't read it without a big lump in my throat or sometimes even tears. Beau was a once-in-a-lifetime kind of horse.

Reunite

The sledgehammer struck without warning or care
Slamming my heart with shock and despair.
Past half-eaten hay and a violated gate
Stared a void that once cradled my chestnut soul mate.

He fearfully foretold what none of us could see
That in the early haze she would take him from me.
Never before had I a connection so deep
Nor a loss, a fall, so severe and jaggedly steep.

Unanswered grasped my letter and frantic calls
Raw and bleak stood his forlorn, empty stall.
For three tortured months tears ruled, then waned
As bruised living trudged on and healing I feigned.

Then in the chills of December I felt his heart
Silently crying to me from dawn to dark.
With fear draped in hope I reached out once more
This time, miraculously, her steely grip tore.

So willingly into the trailer he strode
Like a war-torn soldier, he was going home.
With four prancing feet and two eyes alight
He knew, in short time, we would soon reunite.

Tearfully trembling and soaring with vivid joy
I welcomed him home, my cherished big, red boy.
It was over, our severed life, with its grievous toll
We belong, this horse and I, together one, whole.

FOREVER GOODBYE

I moved back to my hometown in southern Illinois in 2009 to enjoy time with my aging parents. Of course, I took my horses with me. I lived there for five years. In the meantime, Beau's knee kept getting worse and worse. He was getting cast, which basically means stuck laying down, more and more often. It was one emergency after the other. I hadn't been able to ride him for months. He would often struggle for hours until I arrived, found him stuck, and worked to get him up on all fours. This went on every couple weeks, sometimes weekly, for several months before I could let him go. It was so confusing because when he was up, he seemed strong and happy and my usual big, red boy. But I knew he couldn't physically handle the trailer ride from Illinois to Colorado when I moved there in early 2014.

I was driving to the St. Louis airport one morning to fly to LA for a hand analysis workshop when it hit me. It was time. I had to schedule the vet right then, at that moment, or I knew I would lose my nerve. I wanted my other horse to have some time, a month or so, to grieve before moving him alone, without his buddy Beau, across the country again into an entirely new climate and area. I called the vet right then while driving and scheduled Beau's passing the next week.

I have no words to describe watching your beloved horse fall dead to the ground with a huge thud. There is just nothing like it. Somehow those big animals get under your skin deeper than other pets. I always had dogs or cats, and I loved them deeply. I have two cats now I treasure. But horses? Whole different deal.

That week flew by, it didn't matter that I wanted it to drag out. Beau was his calm, stoic self, I was the one buzzing on the inside and trying to keep it together. The country vet, usually very quiet and all business, was completely compassionate and kept telling me what a good horse owner I was and how lucky Beau was to have me as his mom. Then quickly, it was done.

I pulled over on the way home to sob. But not for long. I just couldn't hold onto the sadness. I knew I shoved it down, all that horrible grief, same as I did when my parents died. Well they're supposed to go first, right? They were old, right? Sure Jayne.

HE'S STILL AROUND

To this day Beau still shows up in my life, years after I lost him to that horribly arthritic left knee at the age of twenty-eight.

About eight months after I moved to Denver, nine months after losing Beau, I decided to get another horse to keep Comet company and to ride when Comet was lame or ill. He was growing old, and I knew these instances would occur more frequently. I was trying to determine whether or not to rescue a horse I found at a trail-riding facility in the Colorado foothills just west of Denver. This horse was skeletal. He was so starved, with protruding ribs and hip bones, discolored mane from lack of nutrition, and dejected. Darby seemed like a good horse, but I was experienced enough to know that such a thin horse had no energy and once healthy, could be a completely different animal. I was driving home after the vet check, trying to decide, and was suddenly filled with love rushing through me like I had never felt before.

Chills and chills and chills, the love was so powerful it squeezed tears out of my eyes. "Beau, is that you?" The love and chills increased. "Are you saying Darby is my next horse?" The love increased another notch. I heard him loud and clear. Well, all righty then. I sent as much love as I could back to my big, red boy. At the time, Darby was starving and a skinny, dingy gray Arabian/Appaloosa cross with black polka dots, and a faded black mane and tail. After his health improved and he and I worked through a short adjustment period, he has been wonderful, a super-star in his own right. And he is as handsome as they come. Thank you, Beau.

RELEVANT HAND MARKINGS

THE SCHOOL OF LOVE

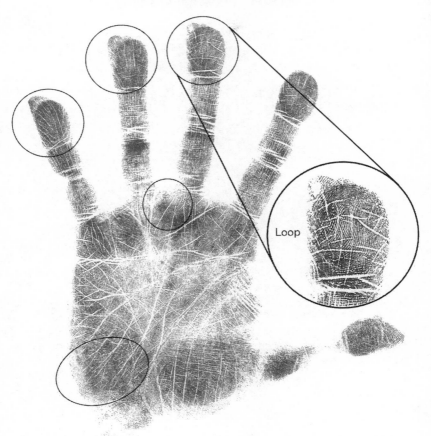

Loop

It may be difficult to see the actual fingerprints, so I have called one out to show you what a loop looks like . . . the loop part of a tied shoelace that doesn't close at the end. It can face any direction, usually to one side or the other. The enlarged loop above opens out to the left.

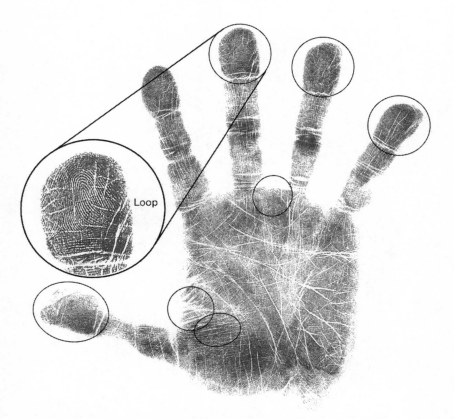

Loop

If you have six or more loop fingerprints, you are in the School of Love, the Path of the Heart. Connections, relationships, closeness and intimacy are the hallmarks of this school.

I am in the School of Love, represented by the number of Loop fingerprints I have in both hands combined. Six are required to be in this school. I have twelve—seven on my fingers and five in my palms, all circled in the images above. (Loops in my palm are very difficult to see here. Please trust they are there.)

Your Life School (or Schools in some cases, like mine, I am also in the School of Service) functions like your operating system, the over-arching energy of your life, or the filter through which you experience life and make decisions. Your school identifies some of your natural skills and talents, as well as some of the learning, or training, you need to fulfill your life purpose.

The aspects of the School of Love that show up in the previous stories include the following:

I am much about love, connection, and relationships. When on the Master path I recognize, honor, and express my feelings regardless of how someone might respond. I am authentic to my emotions, accept them, and above all, practice and live from self-love.

The Student path of this school can look like denying and stuffing emotions, as I did with the grief of losing my beloved horse, not expressing emotions when you feel them, over-giving, avoiding intimacy, fearing loss of love or friendship and making decisions based on that fear, and more.

Are you in the School of Love?

Look at your fingerprints and see if you have loops like I do. Six or more and you are in the School of Love too. Your school is a big element of who you are. Consequently, you and everyone else will be on the Student path in some way frequently. How does this show up for you? If you can recognize it, you can take action to move at least temporarily to the Master path, and that's how we change our lives.

So watch for thoughts and actions including withholding your true emotions, doing what makes other people feel loved instead of what makes you feel self-loved first, stuffing uncomfortable feelings, over-giving, blaming others for how you feel, denying your emotions…anything that is not being responsive to, responsible for, or authentic to your true emotions. Then do your best to turn that around.

LINE OF PERSEPHONE

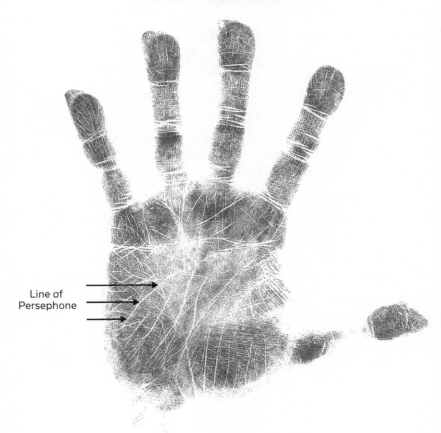

Line of
Persephone

A long head line that curves and dives deeply in the Moon quadrant of the hand, this gift marking is an indication of deep intuitive wisdom.

A Persephone Line is a form of a head line, pointed out in the image above. This long head line dives down into the Moon area, the outer lower quadrant of either hand. Persephone is a Gift Marking.

The short version of the relevant mythology is that Persephone was kidnapped by the god of the Underworld and taken way down deep. She could only come back up once a year to visit her mother. When she came up from the Underworld, she would bring other lost souls with her. So anyone with a Persephone Line is referred to as a guide for lost souls. The Gift is access to deep intuitive wisdom.

One possible characteristic of someone with a Persephone Line is a love for language. Many love poetry, some even enjoy writing poetry. When I'm emotionally motivated, I absolutely love the challenge of finding unusual ways to express my feelings and searching for the perfect word that rhymes while communicating the concept I want to impart.

Some people with Persephone Lines also have a child-like quality to them, love children and vice versa. That describes me as well. I love doing hand analyses for children, teenagers, and young adults. I can relate to them, communicate well with them, and I am always deeply moved how this work gives them confidence and direction for both them and their parents. The Student path? Sudden lethargy, depression, a captured or trapped feeling, just like Persephone felt.

Do you have a Line of Persephone?

Check your head line, the middle major line that starts at the edge of your hand between your index finger and your thumb. Does it go straight across, or curve downward into the Moon area? Do the characteristics described above resonate with you? If so you may have this gift marking. Use it wisely, best with excellent heart-centered listening before offering any of your wisdom.

Beau, My Big Red Boy

CHAPTER 2

MY FEISTY LITTLE SHIT

I bought Comet a year or so after I got Beau. He and Beau were best friends. When his owner decided to sell him, I knew at that time I needed a second horse like I needed a hole in the head, but I couldn't let him be sold to a stranger. I was crazy about Comet. Not only had I known and ridden him many times at Tanya's ranch, but at the new barn, I had nursed him back to health after a terrible accident.

Comet's girth came loose during a gallop up the mountain trail. The saddle, a Peruvian version made with wood and metal bolts, broke apart, slid back, threw off his rider, torqued down over his hips and sliced up his legs as he kicked and ran in a completely hysterical panic at the lion eating his back end.

The boarder called me, breathless, and asked me to come to the barn, as Comet's rider left to get her own injuries cared for. When I arrived the vet walked out to warn me—blood was everywhere. She said his hind legs looked like hamburger. Comet's mom Sherry was a busy attorney and lived too far away to visit regularly, the next day she called to ask me to do my best to rehabilitate her little Paso Fino.

I fell even more in love with the little guy. We got so close, I could walk him down the street with the lead draped over his back, that feisty little shit as I always called him, and he would stay right by my side, until then unheard of behavior for Comet. Even months later, when someone was riding him up the street, he would ease over and tuck in right beside or behind me.

After a few weeks, the bandages and medications could go, but he and I still had a lot of work to do before he could be ridden. It took weeks to get him to accept a saddle again. I started with a little towel and worked my way up. Then I would just walk him down the street with the saddle on. I will admit I was a little nervous the first time I climbed aboard. Comet was an angel. He behaved perfectly. By then he trusted me so much I probably could have put a cougar on the saddle. (Um, not.) Anyway, after a few rides, he was ready for his owner. But our bond was sealed.

I bought him a year or so later when Sherry had to let him go. It was SO the right thing to do for him, for Beau, and turns out, also for me. Once back in Illinois, I taught one niece how to ride on Beau while I rode Comet. He was far too feisty for beginning riders unless he was in the middle or last position in a string of horses. Years had passed since being used as a public riding horse, and he had stepped far away from plodding along on a trail with a beginner on his back.

Feisty was the best word, and if you were comfortable with that, he was a very fun ride. I could aim him anywhere out in the woods and he would go, no argument. He was little enough that I could ride him between tight trees, under branches, and across creeks with obstacles Beau never could have fit through.

Too soon it was Comet's turn to leave the planet. He contracted a terrible disease shortly after we moved to Colorado. It was equine protozoan myeloencephalitis, EPM, caused by protozoa in opossum poop. The critters poop in the fields, which are then harvested for hay. Horses eat the hay, and sometimes if their immune system is compromised, they get EPM. Lesions then grow on the brain and spinal cord, causing physical instability, lameness, possible blindness, and often death.

I was at a conference in Las Vegas when the neighbor called, a new friend I still ride with today. Julie told me Comet was stumbling around backwards in a circle and couldn't stop. Even with that, and with their many years of experience with horses, it took her and my other riding friend Ally forty minutes to catch him in his quarter-acre corral, the feisty little shit. We had only been there a couple months, and he had always been very difficult for anyone other than me to catch. But they finally got him, and I'll be forever grateful to them for keeping an eye on my boy, not giving up the chase, and staying with him that night.

They texted me a video of him stumbling around and had already called the vet. He arrived, took a look, treated Comet with heavy anti-inflammatories and antibiotics. The vet told me Comet was nearly blind and asked me what I thought was wrong. They were thinking he might have somehow sustained a head injury. "I think he's got EPM," I told the vet. I just knew it, and blood tests later confirmed it. The only meds for EPM were about $1,000 a month, and that was out of the question back then. I thought I was going to lose Comet as soon as I got back from Las Vegas.

Then Julie told me about a friend whose horse got EPM and was helped a great deal by an experimental drug developed by a vet in Florida. I tracked the vet down, but she needed my vet in Colorado to order them. Because they did not yet have FDA approval, my vet refused. I dumped him in a heartbeat and switched to one of his partners, a woman who was skeptical but helpful, and got Comet started on those meds, at under $100 a month. Those meds kept him alive for over three years. Another big thank you to Julie for that deeply meaningful referral.

Comet and I bonded even more deeply during his rehabilitation from the acute onset of EPM. I hand-walked him several times a week, sometimes jogging along beside him when it was time for a trot. We both loved those therapy days.

Even though his sight had returned, I couldn't ride him after a year or so, and intermittently at that. He was just too weak, my little guy. Thus, I was looking for another horse and found Darby. He and Darby became fast friends. Actually, Darby adored Comet and looked up to him, metaphorically considering Darby was much taller. They looked like the old Mutt and Jeff comic strip characters walking down the street side by side with their considerable size difference.

In the summer of 2017, I could see my little guy fading. His back end was leaning more often and more precariously to the left. He was grumpy, I knew because of discomfort. He had some good days that Spring before, I was able to ride him a few times, just for ten or fifteen minutes. After a year of not being able to ride him, I was in heaven. So was Comet apparently. Darby had slipped on ice in late January and was lame for several months. So I decided to saddle up Comet and see how he did with just a tiny ride in his quarter-acre enclosure. He was so happy. And so tired after about five minutes.

After a few strength-building short rides in his corral, I took him out on the trail for about ten minutes. He actually cantered up a little hill, tossing his mane, feeling so proud. His joy was palpable, and I was over the moon. The next time we talked with Jan the animal communicator, he started the conversation with, "Jan, did Jayne tell you? I'm her guy again!" I had not yet told her I was riding him. I burst into happy tears.

But the illness took its toll. Later that year he was getting more and more uncomfortable. I checked in with Linda, my new amazing animal communicator here in the Denver area. She said he was indeed in pain and nearly ready to go, but was hanging on because he didn't think I was ready.

I told her to tell him that I would *get* ready, that I had humans to support me and help me work through it, and that I didn't want to be the one keeping him stuck in his body. Animals don't mind when it's their time to go. Other than being killed prematurely by a predator, they're usually good with transitioning when it's time and look forward to their next adventure. So Comet told me through Linda he wanted just another few months to enjoy the sun but that he didn't want to go through another winter. And that he wanted to try being a racehorse in his next life. That so tickled me.

He continued to decline in health, but his spirits were better, I think he was comforted knowing that I would fulfill his wish when it was time. He had said three months, but after two I could tell he was ready to go, I could just sense it. I confirmed with Linda and sure enough, it was time. He had declined more quickly than any of us, including him, anticipated. I scheduled the vet for one week out and spent as much time as I could with Comet during that week. December 1, 2017, was the big day.

Linda texted me that morning to tell me he was calm and happy, and that Beau's spirit was with him. She said it was beautiful. She told me Beau was with me too and was helping Darby as well. It was time. And for the first and only time in his nearly thirty-two years on the planet, that feisty little shit stood rock-still for a needle. He knew it was his release. And once again I watched a beloved horse crash to the ground with an unforgettable and heart-wrenching whump.

Darby grieved longer over Comet than I did. The morning my little guy died, I made sure Darby witnessed the entire process and smelled Comet after his spirit left his body. But even then, for hours afterwards, Darby would run to all four corners of his quarter-acre enclosure, put his head over the fence and whinny so loud his body shook, calling for his dear friend. His grief and loss were hard to watch, to say the least.

Of course, I was stuffing my grief, although I didn't want to. Darby was not himself for several months. He even stopped holding his face against mine in the morning and letting me kiss him on his eyelid or nose, that was our thing. Linda explained that he felt he could never live up to Comet's place in my heart, that Comet was a superstar and Darby knew he was letting me down. Not to mention that he missed Comet dreadfully. I explained to Darby that I needed him to be Darby, that he was just what I was looking for and was a superstar in his own right. That Comet was wonderful, but I was ready for Darby. I saw him visibly relax when Linda told him my feelings. The very next ride, and the vast majority since, have been fabulous.

I had bracelets made from both Beau's and Comet's tails, and I treasure them. I have Comet's on right this minute while typing this story. I am so blessed to have had two such wonderful equine partners. And Darby is the third. My favorite thing in the world is to ride him alone on the trail, just him and me, soaking up nature and each other. It's magical.

RELEVANT HAND MARKINGS

So how does my openness to animal communication show up in my hands? My ability to make the tough life-and-death decisions, and still ride horses after coming off rather frighteningly five times? (Equestrians 'come' off a horse, not 'fall' off. This terminology covers all possibilities of how, such as falling off or getting thrown.) Four of my horse wrecks were caused by dogs off-leash, grrrrr.

LOOP IN MOON, SHAMAN ZONE

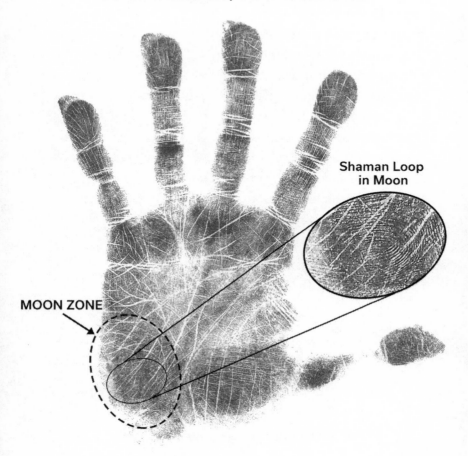

**Shaman Loop
in Moon**

MOON ZONE

This fingerprint, because of its location deep in the Moon, reveals the owner is not only an intuitive guide meant to help people, but also has a connection to animals, the earth, nature, other dimensions.

The fingerprint above, near the outer lower corner of my left palm across from my thumb, is in the Shaman zone of the Moon. The Moon area of the hand represents intuition, other dimensions, and core identity. A fingerprint, in my case a Loop, in the Shaman zone indicates that I'm a coach/counselor and healer. I am designed to help people through a crisis of meaning—any change, transition, event, or situation that is challenging for them and changes their core identity, however mildly. I also have deep connections to nature, the earth, and animals.

The fact that the loop opens to the outside edge of my hand adds to this energy because it's rarer. That, along with other intuitive markings in my hands, helped me to receive Beau's love and message about Darby, know when Beau and Comet were ready to transition, and feel so at home with all kinds of animals.

Do you have a fingerprint in your Moon zone?

In good light, best with a magnifying glass, check the outer lower quadrants of both hands to see if you have a fingerprint in your Moon zone. If so, you are meant to help others through a crisis of meaning as described above. It also means you will experience these crises too, to help you prepare and experience the feelings you are meant to help others through.

The Student path of this marking shows up as disconnection from your intuition. Not recognizing it, or trusting it, nor relying on it. Missing it, ignoring it. When you are disconnected from your intuition, it makes you feel flat, stagnate, disillusioned, even depressed. Remember that Student paths are the yucky feelings in life, the lessons we need to learn and work on to fulfill our purpose and achieve the joy and success we want.

BIG HEART HEARTLINE

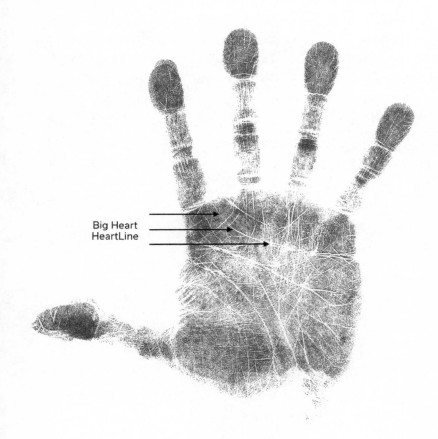

Big Heart
HeartLine

Starting under your pinky, the Big Heart traverses all the way across the top of your palm to, or just inside of, your index finger. It means you have a big heart, motivated to connect, nurture, and help others.

Your heart line, the uppermost major horizontal line across your palms, represents your relationship style—how you communicate in relationships, how you express love and affection to anyone you care for, and how you prefer love and affection to be expressed to you. There are four basic heart line types or relationship styles. The heart line always starts below the pinky and runs across the top of the palm toward the index finger. Where it ends identifies your relationship style. (Keep in mind, I am teaching basics here. I could write an entire book about the four heart lines.)

In short, the Big Heart Master path is all about love, connection, nurturing, and helping others. The Student path shows up as over-giving, finding it difficult to accept help when offered, and not asking for help enough because you want to be the one helping.

My Big Heart shows up in the previous stories as the deep love and connection I have with my friends, my desire to be a volunteer at the ranch and to help with Comet before I owned him. It shows up now as my commitment to help others live their best life by following the blueprint in their hands. My current work is directly and solely about helping people.

MARS STAR AND LOOP FINGERPRINT

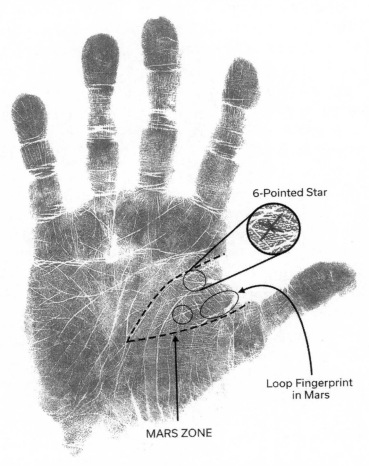

6-Pointed Star

Loop Fingerprint in Mars

MARS ZONE

Any activity in the Mars zone indicates masculine character-istics, such as courage, aggression or assertiveness, taking action and risks, advocating, being protective.

I have several Mars markings. Mars was the god of war, so the Mars area in the hand represents the masculine. Aggres-sion, warrior, courage, and advocacy are Mars characteris-tics. The courage could be physical, emotional, mental, and/

or spiritual. I have a loop fingerprint and a line in Mars in my right hand, and star gift markings in the Mars area of both hands. When I got my first hand analysis, the analyst told me I had exceptional courage. I wasn't aware. I didn't feel particularly brave.

She admonished me, "Jayne, haven't people told you your entire life that you are brave?" Well, now that you mention it, maybe so, I thought. Maybe my skydive, bungee jump, moving across country alone five times, starting two different businesses, getting divorced twice, coming out of the spiritual metaphysical closet after being raised Catholic in a small southern Midwest town, riding horses so fast it felt like I had to bend forward against the wind so as not to get blown off...you mean stuff like that?

Okay, I get it now, I see it. Sometimes a gift is such a natural part of who we are that it is easy to overlook and not embrace or use intentionally. Often, I have to remind my clients with Mars markings of how bravery can show up in their lives so they can see it, recognize it, own it, and access it.

Several aspects of the previous story are relevant to Mars markings. One is, making the courageous decision to put down my horse without waiting for a horrible emergency to make the decision for me. Riding horses, to begin with, is another, and I mean riding, baby. My friends and I would haul ass up mountain trails, whipping around corners on our horses so fast we had to grab mane, hunker down to lower our center of gravity and lean into the turns.

More than once I've had to direct a runaway horse—meaning one who took the bit in its teeth and was having a little too much fun running as fast as it possibly could—into tall bushes alongside the trail. In those situations, the preferred way to stop a runaway horse, turning their head to the side without turning their body very much, was risky due to narrow trails along mountainsides. Heart-pounding exhilaration for sure. And scratches from bushes, but that sure beats coming off and bouncing on a hard-packed dirt trail with rocks everywhere. Tanya had only a couple horses that would take the bit in their teeth and run full out, usually only when ridden alone. So let's say I knew the risks when I rode these speed demons and did it anyway. I have learned there is a lot of courage in ignorance. If you don't know what could go wrong, you won't be afraid of it.

Mars Master path also involves advocacy, standing up for the underdog, being protective of and fighting for loved ones. Boy oh boy do I ever advocate. It seems like it just happens. One minute I'm minding my own business, the next I become aware of an injustice or threat to someone or something I love, and look out here I come. I am known to sometimes fight for people and situations I'm not connected to as well, it only takes seeing the unfairness and threat of harm to propel me to action.

One example of how I experienced the Student path of Mars showed up after I came off a horse one of my boyfriends and I owned. Sedona was a pretty thoroughbred, young and inexperienced on the trail. One of the sayings among horse people is "Green on green equals black on blue," referring to an inexperienced or green rider on an inexperienced or green horse often leading to deep bruises or worse for the rider. Well, that was me at the time on Sedona. And, the first of several times I came off a horse spooked by a dog off-leash chasing them in a threatening manner. Anyway, it was a scary fall, and although I didn't break any bones, I was hurt enough that I couldn't ride for a few months. The fright of that experience kept me from riding my usual favorites at the barn. Once I healed, I was too afraid to ride the more energetic or challenging horses and would only ride what I called baby horses—those reserved for beginner riders. It took me several weeks to get my nerve up to return to my standbys. But Master path—I did get back in the saddle with those guys, figuratively and literally.

Do you have extra courage?

Do you have a six-pointed star in the Mars area of either hand? If so, you have the capacity for extra courage as well, for taking action and advocating for the underdog. It also means, just like me, you will experience the Student path too, which shows up as not using your courage, staying on the cowardice end, not taking action you know you need to take, and/or not advocating. It can also manifest as anger issues (a masculine emotion).

BIG FINGERTIPS

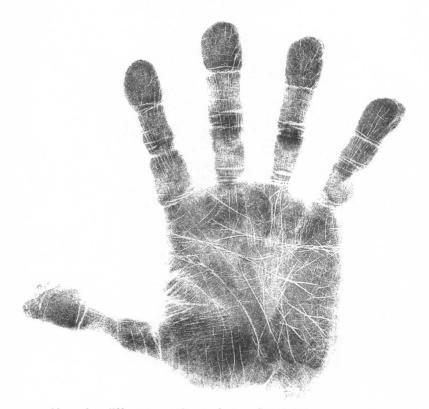

How the different sections of your fingers show up and compare to the other sections means something, depending on the specific finger and the specific section. If most of your fingertips are larger than other finger zones, you likely have an affinity for things philosophical, spiritual, scientific, abstract, or metaphysical.

Notice in the image above how large the top zones of my fingers are compared to the other sections. This indicates an affinity for things philosophical, spiritual, scientific, and metaphysical. Combine my Shaman fingerprint with these large top zones, and I'm definitely attracted to things spiritual and metaphysical, such as animal communication. Interestingly, I also have long, straight head lines indicating I'm logical and analytical, as well as a few whorl fingerprints revealing I can be very mental and in my head. These characteristics both complement and oppose each other.

Speaking of metaphysics and Comet—this happened the day I submitted my manuscript for printing . . . hard core skeptics may want to turn the page.

James van Praagh is likely the most renowned psychic medium in the world due in large part to his amazing accuracy. Mediums have the ability to communicate with people and animals who have passed. James has been on many television talk shows, written multiple books, was the expert on the TV series Ghost Whisperer, and more.

Mile Hi Church here in Denver hosted an event with James in June 2019. There were at least 300 people in the audience, all hoping they would hear from a loved one. I have had individual sessions with mediums, during which my mom, dad, grandfather, and dear friend Flossie who passed in 2011, the one who introduced me to animal communication, came through to bring me loving messages. It's a wonderful experience, extremely soul-satisfying, comforting, and emotional in the highest sense of the word. I've also attended several gallery readings, similar to the one at Mile Hi, with large groups.

So here I am at the Mile Hi event, silently asking my mom to try to get through the clutter of many spirits wanting to be heard, and talk with me. The closure and comfort James brought to some of the audience members was palpable and highly moving. It was time for his last reading of the night. "This one is a little different," James said. "I have a four-legged loved one coming through. It's a horse." My ears perked up.

Long story a little less long, it was Comet, for me. Standing at my seat, holding the microphone a runner handed me and with tears welling up, I listened to James as he shared what he heard from Comet and saw psychically. All of it was freaky accurate. Here are the main elements, with my explanations in parentheses:

He said Comet knew I saved him when he hurt his legs so badly. That he greatly appreciated my constant care and devotion, and that he loved me more than I know. That when he got sick I brought in a specialist (the vet in Florida), and he knew that helped him live longer. That he was always with me, and saw that I did something with his blanket recently (I donated it to a horse rescue a couple months ago), and that I still had his bridle and saddle but wasn't using them. Comet said his passing was peaceful (it was the first time he didn't freak out about a getting a shot), but he knew it was an excruciating decision for me. James said Comet would be bringing me another horse. (We'll see how that part goes, I have no interest in a second horse at this time, I am so enjoying Darby and the convenience of owning only one horse. But neither can I predict the future.)

Then James said sometimes animals have trouble breaking through strongly enough for mediums to pick up their communication, especially in a gallery situation, and that they often need people who have passed to help them.

James told me that my dad is the one who helped Comet come through. That it was my dad's way to demonstrate his love for me since he didn't know how to do that very well while he was alive.

Holy moly, what an experience. I am so grateful to my dad, to Comet, and of course to James, for this unforgettable and deeply profound communication. And as I write this chapter's addendum of sorts, the realization hit me that another WHY for this book, another mission of mine, is to open more people up to the spiritual metaphysical world and all it has to offer.

Comet in his feisty days

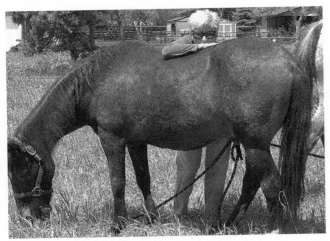

Jayne with 30-year-old Comet

CHAPTER 3

FAIRIES, FORTS, and FLYING

I knew they were there and could sense them, the little fairies in the woods. I never saw or heard them. I just knew they were there. They were not my child's imagination, I am convinced. (And here's where some of my acquaintances may slowly back away with skeptical fear in their eyes—I've seen a few while walking along Bear Creek here in Denver too.) I believe that some instances of imagination are often actually real, including many children's relationships with imaginary friends. This is one of the reasons I loved being in the woods by myself when I was a kid. I loved sitting near the creek under the big tree whose branches swept the ground to form a hideout, a very special place. I think the fairies came to keep me company, even though I never felt lonely as a child. Hello, maybe because fairies were with me.

I also loved stomping down a secret 'house' in the tall grass in the field between the two big patches of woods behind our house. Then I would lie down in this second special place and watch the clouds. I could always find shapes of things and animals in the clouds. Once while 'clearing a room' in the tall weeds, I stepped on a garter snake which immediately wrapped itself around my ankle. It startled me, but I've never been afraid of snakes. It unwound and slithered away before I could catch it, darn it. So I ran home and dragged my brother out to help me. I led him to where I had experienced my snake encounter, stepped down to show him how it happened, and holy moly the snake wrapped around my ankle again. This time, we caught it. I always let my captured critters go free after I enjoyed their company for a few days or weeks. They were my friends after all, and they deserved their freedom.

One day while enjoying my secret little grass house with no roof, a calico cat came wandering in and curled up a few feet away. I welcomed it, but sensed it was best not to try to pet it. After about an hour, it got up and sauntered away. That cat came every day I visited my special place, curling up closer and closer to me, eventually stepping gingerly into my lap and taking a little snooze. He/she was my little friend that no one else knew about. I felt very special.

One day it didn't show up, and I never saw it again. A house in the neighborhood had burned down recently, and I feared it may have been trapped inside, but I have no idea. I watched for it with tentative hope every time I visited my secret house.

I caught just about anything that moved, other than bugs and spiders, yuck, with lightning bugs being the one exception. I captured turtles, mudpuppies, snakes, lizards, salamanders, a baby bird, a baby duck, a baby bunny, even a bat with my brother's help. That last one didn't stay around long. My mom nearly had a heart attack when she caught sight of that critter, which was released immediately.

Animals, alive or stuffed, were a big part of my young life, and continue to be. I would pull every encyclopedia (I know, I'm aging myself) one by one off the shelf in the family room, look for color photos of any animals, and pour over them repeatedly. I dreamed of having my own dog in my own house that I didn't have to share with a big family or keep outside. I wanted it to sleep with me. And my biggest dream? My own horse.

Thirty years later that dream finally came true. Never give up. I have so many horse stories that impacted me deeply and added lovely tapestry to my life. More stories are being added to that mosaic every year.

Children are born connected to their spiritual and psychic abilities. Society, well-meaning and/or frightened parents, and sometimes children's own fears are what cause blocks and stuffing down those connections. Once when young, probably five or six years old, one night after I fell asleep I flew down the stairs and around our home. It was glorious.

The next day I excitedly told my mom, and she looked at me with thinly disguised skepticism and said, "Hmmm, really? That's nice honey."

As I look back, it was wonderful that she didn't scold me or demand that I never speak of such things again. I now know it was astral travel, an out-of-body experience. I have been waiting for a repeat performance ever since. Have you ever awakened with a start so suddenly that you jumped out of your sleep? Not as a result of a dream, but you didn't know what caused the jump? The short version is that you, your spirit, was out of your body and basically slammed back in. I know, weird, right? I can feel some of you raising your eyebrows with skepticism, and that's okay, I get it.

GAIL THE PSYCHIC

Even before my connection with animal communicators, I had dipped my toe in the water metaphysically when I was living in NYC. During my second career, my boss had transferred me there, and I was thrilled. I had traveled to NYC many times on business and loved the energy of that amazing city. But I couldn't ignore the fact that, after several years doing sales and marketing for a big graphics design firm, I was miserable in my work.

Not with the company itself, but with working so hard. Mostly I knew at some level I was meant to do something else. I felt unfulfilled, bored and off-track, and it was driving me crazy. As much as I cared for and respected my boss Kevin and the company, I sensed there was other work I was meant to do, I just had no idea what. Seeing a career coach did not help, nor did all the books I read about finding your passion and ideal work. At least they didn't work for me.

I was complaining once again to Stan, my boyfriend at the time about how lost I felt. He said, "I have a friend who could help you."

I answered, "Another career coach?" He explained no, she was a psychic.

I looked at him in complete skepticism. "Are you serious?"

He smiled as if he had heard this kind of reaction before. "What have you got to lose? Aren't you curious?" He had a point. Actually, two points.

So I called Gail, half-relieved her name wasn't Starlight or Fortuna or Infinity. At the time of the phone appointment, I sat in my living room in my New York City apartment, while she was in Southern California. She started the session by saying, "Okay, let me tune in here. I see lots of peach, soft blue, sea foam green, and cream around you. Does that mean anything?"

The hair stood up on the back of my neck. Chills raced up and down my spine. My walls were painted peach, and the southwestern style chaise I sat on was peach, soft blue, sea foam green, and cream. Gail had my attention. (And no, oh fellow skeptical ones, Stan lived in Colorado and had not yet been to my apartment in NYC. He couldn't have revealed to her my color scheme.)

She told me I would eventually start my own business. Until that moment, doing so had never crossed my mind. That would be way too scary.

Using her input, while slowly, and I mean slowly, healing from an unexpected illness shortly after my return to LA from NYC, I decided to start a speaking business. Making presentations had been my favorite part of both of my previous careers. It just made sense. If I had known before I started how long it would take me to make a living from it, I would have never had the nerve to do it. Thank goodness, I didn't know.

After my experience with Gail, the psychic, I felt I had a dark secret. Me, metaphysical?! What in the world would people think of me now? I couldn't tell anyone for months. One day I was having lunch with a friend from work at a favorite New York City restaurant near Union Square. I blurted out, "Sal, you won't believe what I did. I talked with a psychic." Without looking up from her pasta, Sal replied, "Great! I have a wonderful astrologer you should talk to. You would love it."

And just like that, many—but not all—of my fears of being seen as weird were put to rest. The more I opened up about my foray into metaphysics, the more people I found were already there.

Years later, when I moved back to my hometown to spend time with my parents, I talked to my mom about it and kept her updated about my experiences. She never specifically said she believed it, but I knew she had experienced her own versions of such things and couldn't find fault with my exploration. I could tell she was fascinated.

My mom told me that more than twenty years earlier, as she was on her way to see her dad in the hospital before his heart surgery, she felt his spirit go right through her and knew he was gone. Sure enough, the hospital confirmed he died at the same time she felt him pass through her.

RELEVANT HAND MARKINGS

IMAGE OF UPPER FINGER ZONES

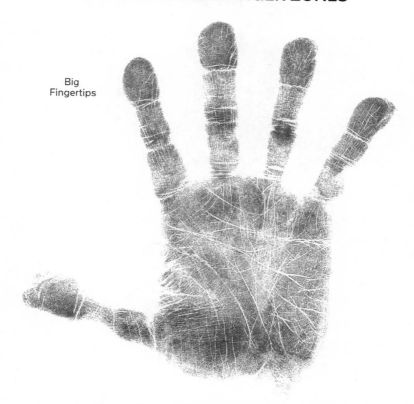

Big
Fingertips

When the top zone of the fingers looks larger than the other sections respectively, the person likely is attracted to things spiritual, metaphysical, philosophical, abstract.

As I mentioned previously, the upper zones of my fingers are larger and longer than average, indicating an attraction to or affinity for things spiritual, philosophical, abstract, scientific, and metaphysical.

MERCURY LINE

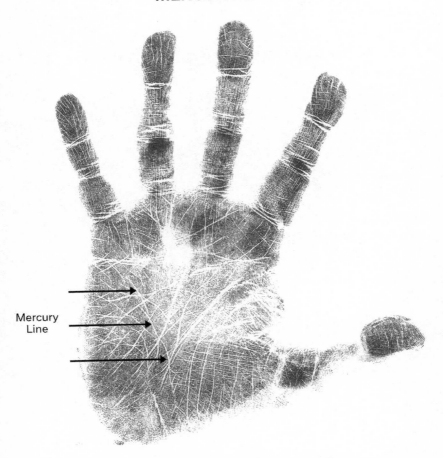

Mercury
Line

A Mercury line indicates a search for spiritual understanding and place in the world, asking the big questions about God and related beliefs.

I have a Mercury line, also called the spiritual seeker, which indicates I am a searcher for things and connections Divine. I've asked the big questions—what are my spiritual beliefs, just who or what is God? On the Master path, spiritual seekers have a two-way channel with the Divine. If I ask a question of God, Spirit, Source, my higher power, the answer will come. It's my job to be tuned in to hear it and watch for signs. God will try to get the answer to us any way He can, including words in our head, a feeling in our body, an article in a magazine, even a conversation behind us in the coffee shop.

I have a fingerprint in the Moon zone, specifically the Shaman zone. Part of who I am is a spiritual teacher meant to help others through a crisis of meaning and core identity issues. It also means I have the ability to connect with other dimensions, and will experience my own core identity changes and challenges off and on. Boy does that explain a lot. Most of which is not in this book or it would be 1,000 pages long.

LINE OF CLAIRVOYANCE, MOON STAR

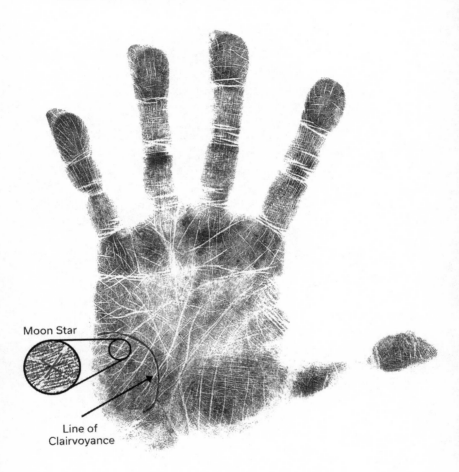

Moon Star

Line of
Clairvoyance

These are intuitive gift markings, revealing an ability to connect with intuition often and powerfully. The Moon Star indicates flashes of intuition, the Line of Clairvoyance on the Master path has constant access.

I also have several intuitive gift markings (two of them are shown above), so when on the Master path I am connected to intuition, even to psychic abilities. I'm working on capturing the flow for these. I do struggle with the off and on intuitive disconnection aspect of the Student path, and I'm challenged by my conflicting markings that keep me in my head too easily and too often. My intuition clicks in much more readily when I am coaching my clients than for myself.

Do you listen to your gut?

Are you aware of and connected to your intuition? Your gut instinct? Check your hands to see if you have any of these markings described above. With or without intuitive markings, anyone can benefit from working on their intuition. There are hundreds of books with exercises to help open up these skills, along with classes, webinars, and other programs.

Two simple activities that can be very helpful with this are meditating and keeping an intuition journal. Meditation helps you practice keeping your mind quiet so that when intuition speaks up, it will be easier for you to hear it. Your mind will wander, that's perfectly normal. Just gently pull your attention back to the music or breathing or mantra you are focusing on, and continue.

An intuition journal is short and simple as well. At the end of each day, make a simple note about an event or instance you felt may have been intuitive, how you responded, and what the outcome was. What you focus on will expand is a key principle of the Law of Attraction. Perfect example—one day several years ago I got a tiny wisp of a thought, so easy to ignore, a warning to be careful with my cell phone. PPPFFTTT, I thought to myself, I'm not going to drop my phone. Five seconds later it was literally in the toilet. So that's what intuition felt like for me, ah-ha. Practically nothing, a very quiet and subtle sort-of-thought, less than a whisper. That night in my journal I wrote, "Got a warning about my cell phone, ignored it, lost my cell phone." The more attention you give your intuition, the more you will become aware of it, recognize it, and trust it.

CHAPTER 4

PUSHING THEN CRASHING

This story demonstrates several possible and very challenging manifestations of being stuck on Student paths. Big time. And subsequent events as well, resulting from Student path behavior. Ugh.

I quickly became bored in my first career selling and marketing products in the food industry. The company I worked for was full of wonderful people, it was a great place to work, but I was not cut out for a corporate environment. Too many rules for me, too many layers of bosses, too little freedom. It just took me a few years to figure that out. They moved me to Los Angeles, paid for my MBA, and promoted me quickly up the ranks to product manager within a few short years. But honestly I wasn't that great at it, and elements of that job, such as the detail work, managing people, and the same freedom restrictions I mentioned previously, drove me nuts. Plus, I looked ahead to the next position up the ladder and knew I didn't want it as it would only bring more of the same, only amplified.

So I left and got a great job as head of sales and marketing for a high-level graphics design firm that worked with the Fortune 1000 as clients. I enjoyed a great deal of travel with this job and made sales and design presentations to many packaged goods companies. It was fun. After a few years, I moved to a second graphics company as SVP of sales and marketing. Kevin, the owner of that company, was the best boss I ever had. I loved working for and with him. Kevin was generous and fun with a hands-off management style. For the first few years, I was flying high. This was the job I had when transferred to New York City. I lasted a year, that place wore me out and was just too much input for my sensitive system. Too many people, too much noise, too much grime. But I loved the experience and was so grateful to Kevin for the opportunity. He moved me back to LA, and I continued my work.

The economy fell about that time, and I was working extremely hard. I was the only salesperson and felt the future of that company was on my shoulders.

I also was playing hard, riding horses, scuba diving, running—it seemed like I had every minute planned with a sixty-miles-per-hour daily life. The stress I put on myself to bring in design projects, added to the company's mild pressure on me, was enormous. I was loyal to Kevin and wanted to do my best for him. Plus, I'm naturally a high-achiever, and the thought of the company going under because I didn't bring in enough business was terrifying and completely unacceptable to me.

Before long, I suffered from horrible headaches every day and stopped getting up early to exercise. I was deeply, completely beaten to a pulp. Big clues I ignored. During a business trip we made to Minneapolis, Kevin could see my utter exhaustion. After our big presentation, in the car headed back to the airport, I could barely reach my arm out to pick up my cup of water out of the cup holder.

"Jayne, I think you have Epstein-Barr," he said. "I had it several years ago. I want you to go see my Chinese doctor."

So I did. Kevin's doctor told me I had both Epstein-Barr and Chronic Fatigue Syndrome, so severely that I would crash for a year if I didn't stop my life.

Well, that seemed ridiculous to me. Being so active and Mars-like, I just couldn't relate to such a warning. I took a week off and spent a wonderful week in Yosemite, partly alone and partly with my boyfriend at the time who lived in San Francisco.

When I returned, the pressure was really on from all fronts to bring in more business. I was getting so sick that Kevin gave me Fridays off, but by then I was beyond repair. I was getting sicker and more exhausted by the week. Finally, I pulled in a million-dollar client. Then I crashed head-on.

The doctor was wrong. I didn't lose a year of my life. I lost two.

I went out on disability for as long as that lasted, a few months, then Kevin officially fired me, so that I could earn unemployment. But all that was way too little and stopped way too soon.

I am not exaggerating when I say that brushing my teeth was a major project. I stayed with my parents back in Illinois for a month and should have stayed longer. But no, I'm much too tough (read, hard-headed) for that. I could see my mom was worried.

I didn't feel literally depressed while I was sick, I was too deeply tired to feel anything emotional. I always knew, and held onto, the fact that the disease is not terminal. Clearly, I had stopped all the fun parts of my life. No more horses, scuba, running, partying. I just sat in a chair. I couldn't imagine doing any of those things, and in some weird way that kept me from missing them. After several months, I could at least watch a movie. Eventually, I could read for thirty minutes at a time, then an hour. I was drawn to spiritual books and began to devour them, yearning to understand the meaning behind the trajectory of my life.

Constant rest, which meant sitting on my butt or laying on the sofa, combined with Chinese herbs and soups made from bird nests, as I called them, got me through it. My house smelled like those herbs, boiled with all kinds of things that looked like you would find them as part of a bird's nest or on the forest floor. I never did get used to the odor or the taste, and when I say UGH, I mean double UGH.

Almost three decades later, I still struggle with CFS relapses. They are far fewer and far less severe than the first ten years, but I have to be mindful about my mental energy expenditure combined with physical output. I can always feel them coming, although it took me a few years to figure out what those signs meant. I get a unique kind of headache, a foggy brain, and here's the really weird symptom—my face feels like it wants to slide off my skull. That is the only way I can describe it. And once my face starts sliding, I have to stop my life.

For the first few years, the relapses would last a month or two. Then a couple of weeks. Now they are rare, and I can stop them in their tracks and pull out within a few days.

This challenging experience with long-term illness led me to question everything. It resulted in several of the major experiences of my life and opening up more intentionally to metaphysics.

RELEVANT HAND MARKINGS

MARS STAR AND PRINT

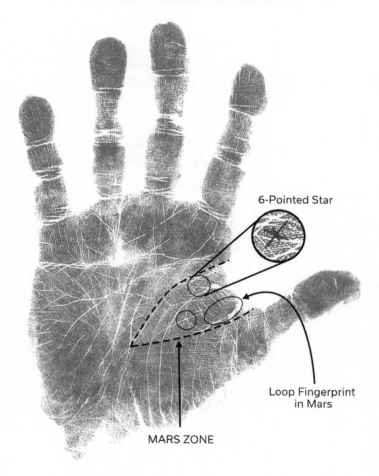

6-Pointed Star

Loop Fingerprint
in Mars

MARS ZONE

Any six-pointed stars or fingerprints in the Mars area
uncover a connection on the Master path to courage,
action, warrior-like protection and advocacy.

The Mars area in the hands represents the masculine—aggression, courage, action, and advocacy. I discussed this in depth after chapter two, but this situation highlights one of the Student paths. I stayed in the warrior way too long. I did not rest enough. Instead, I continually used my masculine energy and kept pushing and pushing. I did not use my feminine side and Venus Star and fingerprint to nurture myself, rest more, and slow down when my head first started aching.

BIG THUMB

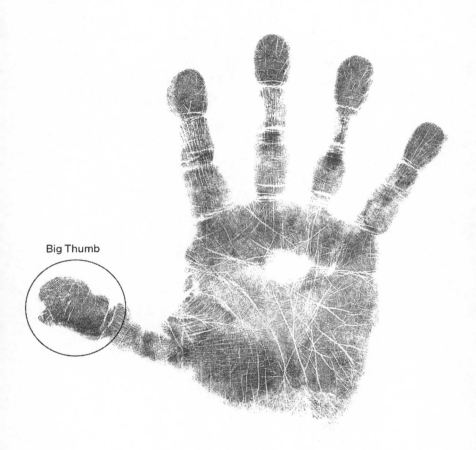

Big Thumb

Thumbs are about intention, will, and an ability to get things done. A strong thumb indicates strong capabilities in these areas.

Notice how the top joint of my thumb is very large compared to the rest of that digit. This thumb pad indicates a strong will and ability to set intentions and get things done. If very large, the person may be a bully, pushy, overbearing.

Threading with my Mars warrior characteristics, my big thumb reveals my ability to impose my will and strong intention to achieve my goals and help my coaching clients achieve their goals. When I'm on the Master path, I'm more in balance and nurture myself more mindfully. The Student path leads me to over-doing. Hello.

JUPITER STAR

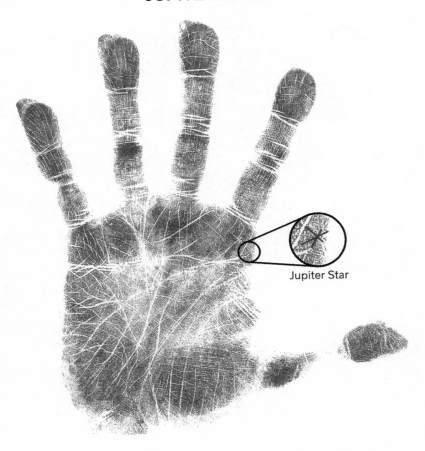

Jupiter Star

A six-pointed star in the mound below the index finger shows the capacity for leadership, drive, and power.

This star below my index finger reveals my capacity, on the Master path, for power, influence, drive, achievement, and leadership. I was on the Student path in this situation...being over-the-top driven and achieving at any cost to myself, not being a good leader for myself.

Are you leading yourself?

My hope is that my experiences are encouraging you to check in with yourself…are you being a good leader for your own life? How so? If not, what does that look like, and what price are you paying?

Are your masculine and feminine aspects in balance? Are you taking action and nurturing yourself at the same time? What steps could you take to do a more effective job of this?

CHAPTER 5

HITTING BOTTOM

The decade between 1987 and 1997 was brutal for me.

Not every day, not every year. That said, those ten years saw me experiencing divorce, a two-year life-as-I-knew-it-stopping illness, losing my beloved home, and filing for bankruptcy.

I was not prepared financially in my mid-thirties for being out of work for two years. Ironically, when I got divorced a few years prior to my illness, my attorney tried to talk me into getting spousal support because my husband made so much more income than I did. I just wouldn't hear of it. Asking my soon-to-be-ex to give me money, other than splitting our assets earned during the marriage, didn't make sense to me. Now, if he had been an awful person or cheated or beat me, different story, different divorce agreement.

But he wasn't awful. We just weren't a good match. He was laid back whereas, as you can tell by now, I'm anything but. On the rare occasions when fighting would have helped to clear the air, and for me to feel expressed and heard, he just couldn't do it. I remember bringing something up one day in the car that I needed to talk about it, and he reached over and turned up the radio. Clearly, I hadn't done a good job of communicating my upset. If that happened today, I would get out of the car at the next light after a few choice words. Instead, I just sat there hurt and steaming. We both had intimacy issues. The good part? We were great friends and really enjoyed each other's company. We spent a lot of time together, by choice. He was, for the most part, a real sweetheart. But I was miserable. I didn't feel loved, seen, or attractive. I couldn't be myself and didn't even understand that at the time.

I was scared to get divorced, for sure, but was also earning a decent income working for Kevin. My attorney asked, "but what happens if you get sick or hurt and can't work?"

I poo-pooed that possibility. "First of all," I responded while trying not to roll my eyes, "that will never happen. And secondly, it wouldn't be his responsibility anyway if we're not married anymore."

"Well," he told me, "I'll put in a loophole in case you change your mind later."

Well, I have big thumbs and a Jupiter star, remember? I can be willful and I'm a high-achiever. I was young and way too naïve to believe anything like long-term disability could ever happen to me. I chose not to use the loophole after I got sick. I still feel it wasn't my ex's responsibility to support me financially just because I got sick. He's not the one who made me sick. I was.

Anyway, interest rates in the early '90s were ridiculously high. My mortgage payment was around $2,500 a month. My savings dwindled very quickly.

During the second year of my illness, I started the speaking business that Gail my psychic friend saw several years earlier. It did make sense to me at the time, as I loved giving sales and design presentations while working for Kevin. It just took a while, and being forced out of my sales and marketing work by illness, to make that leap. My primary topic was gender communication differences in the workplace, and I wrote a book about that titled *GenderSmart—Solving The Communication Puzzle Between Men and Women*. I added a few more topics as well that clients requested as years went by.

That business took several years to get traction. My first year, I brought in a whopping $7,000 in revenue. After a while, I was using credit cards to pay my bills, including my mortgage. I'm sure you can see where this is going.

I listed my townhouse, which I dearly loved, for sale but the recession in the real estate industry had taken hold. It just wouldn't sell. I finally did a short-pay with the bank, which broke my heart for two reasons. Not only did I lose my beloved home, but also my 800-plus credit rating took a nasty dive. I felt shame, grief, embarrassment, and great loss.

I cut my monthly housing expenses by more than half when I moved into an apartment. Not even that was enough. Eventually, I was over $60,000 in credit card debt. I agonized for weeks about filing for bankruptcy. It just felt awful. I felt like a huge failure, a flake. A nine-to-five job was not an option yet. I couldn't work those hours due to my CFS, and a part-time minimum-wage job wouldn't make a big enough difference, I had dug too deep a hole for that. I consulted several experts and all unanimously recommended bankruptcy. So I buried, stomped on, and gulped down my pride and did it. I've made great progress, but I'm still working through remnants of the shame.

Medical-related bankruptcies are common, but the statistics are fuzzy at best. From what I can tell, a classic medical bankruptcy is caused by high medical bills. Many bankruptcies are caused by loss of income after a medical event, like mine. My shame was largely a result of my high expectations of myself, social norms, and my tendency, although lesser now, to beat myself up when I wasn't close enough to perfect.

I've worked on this shame and guilt with therapists, healers, and a focus on personal growth. I've learned to drastically reduce, but not eliminate, self-criticism and being mean to myself. I finally am able to give myself a break without feeling like I am clinging to excuses. I was young, naïve, and did the best I could at the time. I learned that few people in their early thirties could survive on their own two full years with no income other than paltry disability payments. Even so, occasionally I still shake my head in disbelief and sadness about it, and yes a little bit of shame.

RELEVANT HAND MARKINGS

HERMIT HEART LINE

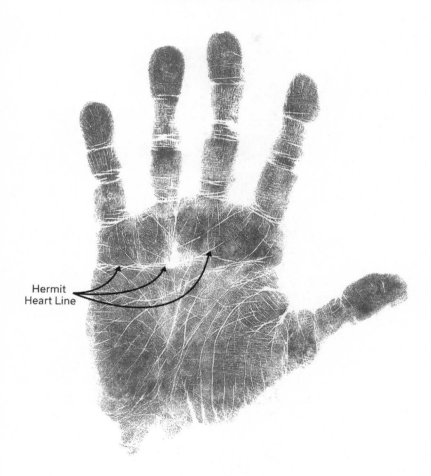

Hermit
Heart Line

One of four possible relationship styles, the Hermit indicates, on the Master path, characteristics of loyalty, integrity, reliability, along with a need for solitary time, space
and freedom.

One Master path aspect of the Hermit heart line, or relationship style, is high integrity. Asking for spousal support when I was perfectly capable of earning a living seemed in conflict with my integrity. No, I wouldn't have the same level of lifestyle as before, but that was a worthwhile trade for my freedom from an unhappy marriage. That integrity is also a large aspect of what made filing for bankruptcy so difficult.

FINGERPRINT BETWEEN
MIDDLE/RING FINGERS, RIGHT HAND

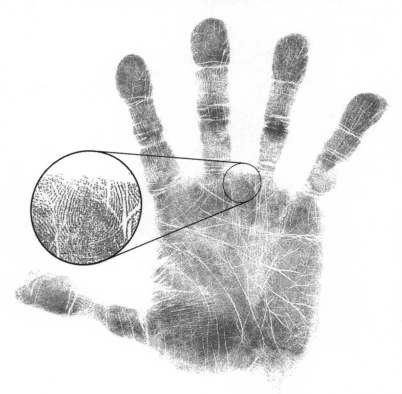

When a fingerprint appears at the top of the palm between two fingers, the meaning of the two fingers are combined to describe what it means. In this case, the middle finger is about business, systems, responsibility, and value. The ring finger indicates creativity.

More than half of my clients have one or more fingerprints in their palms. I have six, one of them being at the top of my right palm in between my middle (Saturn) and ring (Apollo) fingers.

One of the descriptions of the Master path of this particular print is referred to as Using Creativity in Business. I do that, although I'm working on increasing the application of my innovative thinking in my work. I write, speak, create programs, solve client problems, and more.

The Student path is called Challenges Managing Resources, with resources being one or more of time, money, people, information, things, etc. So, there you go. How do I take action on this one? Put a budget into place, save money, carefully consider expenditures, and plan for the unexpected. And most certainly, make self-care a priority. Your most valuable resource is yourself.

PLUTO STAR

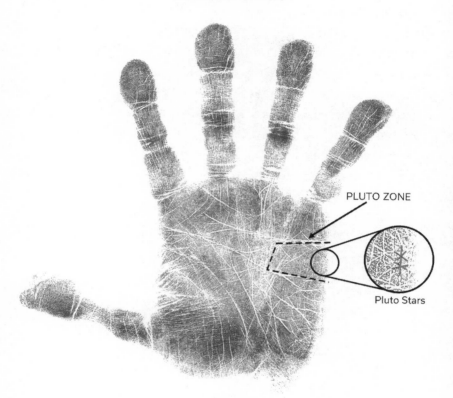

PLUTO ZONE

Pluto Stars

The visual concept for Pluto in the hands is the Phoenix rising from the ashes, indicating death and rebirth.

The owner of a Pluto Star gift marking is a radical transformer, meant to help others face and experience their own change, growth, and radical transformation. To change deeply, something hidden has to be brought up in order to be released. This could be a belief, behavior, thought, relationship, business, or more. A radical transformer on the Master path would not be afraid to climb into someone's stuff, their darkness, to shine a light and bring up for processing what needs to be released.

Here is the kicker—with any and all gift markings, owners will experience the challenge of their specific gifts, so they are better equipped to help others through similar experiences. So with my Pluto Star, I experienced radical transformation. And will again. Divorce, major illness, losing my home, and bankruptcy are all examples of radical transformation. And, because of these experiences, I am more capable of helping others through their deep change and growth. I do this primarily by guiding them into purpose and onto the Master paths of their gifts. I am not a therapist.

Are you a radical transformer?

Have you experienced life events that could be categorized as radical, similar to mine? If so, look closely at the Pluto area of both hands as you may have qualifying markings. Check for a six-pointed star, usually rather small in this area, or multiple vertical lines, lots of activity in the zone. The Pluto zone is the only area in the hands where a lot of vertical activity qualifies as the gift marking for being a radical transformer.

CHAPTER 6

I'M NOT SO GOOD AT THIS —YET

I've been divorced twice. I still find that shocking as I read what I just wrote. Sure never saw that coming in my younger years. You could say that marriage is not my strong suit, at least not yet. I'm still learning how to discern who is a good match for me and vice versa. My hands reveal that I have a great need for freedom, am highly independent and a leader. I need to have great respect for myself and anyone with whom I associate for any length of time or depth of connection. And, I have challenges accessing and trusting my intuition. This last Student path is the biggie.

With both relationships, I got warnings early on that were too easy for me to ignore—the Student path of many intuitive markings. I was twenty-seven when I married a coworker at my first full-time job. He was sweet, loving, intelligent, etc., etc. Even though we dated exclusively and nearly every day for two years before we married, after three short years as husband and wife I was miserable.

I had heard the tiny, quiet warnings of a non-fit before we got married, but told myself I was just nervous and that I could make it work, and that those little things weren't important. Ha. Even when deeply unhappy for a couple of years, I still tried to make it last. The thought of divorce scared the crap out of me and made me feel like a total failure. I had to make it work. We went to counseling together, which helped just a little, for a short while. Then I went by myself.

When I told my husband I was unhappy, he said, "Well darling, I'm happy, so if you're unhappy, figure it out." Nice. So that's what I tried to do.

I didn't know way back then, in the mid-eighties, that a big challenge I have, the Student path of the foundation of my purpose, involves giving my power away. I was undoubtedly on the Student path then. My husband was a conflict-avoider, and I didn't speak up or truly put my foot down when I felt ignored and disrespected. I started avoiding conflict too so as not to upset him. I did go to counseling again, alone, to help me make the decision whether or not to stay. Counseling said leave. The therapist explained that I was fighting a no-win battle and that unless I could get to a place where the relationship as it was worked for me, I would always be miserable. Neither my husband nor I could, or should, change enough to matter.

Big yikes. I was raised Catholic. They don't believe in divorce. At least they didn't back then. I have no idea what their position on that is now. Even though I had stopped participating in the church after I left home for college, it really bothered me. I feared my parents would be devastated. I worried about being judged by everyone else. Any time before then, when I heard about someone getting divorced, I always wondered what they did wrong to screw up their marriage. I was so judgmental and just knew nothing like that could ever happen to me. Now it was my turn—karma at its best. Again, I felt like a failure. I felt shame, and I felt like I had made a huge mistake by marrying the wrong person for me.

Making the final decision took months and months. I did not want to hurt my husband. He truly was a good man. But I couldn't take it anymore. I was being strangled by shoving down my authenticity and living with someone who wasn't right for me nor me right for him. I finally got up the nerve to tell him, and it was over. We remained friends, even stayed in the same house together for six months until it sold.

Afterward, we happened to move back to the same neighborhood we lived in while dating. We took care of each other's kitties when we traveled. I always invited him to any party I planned. Eventually, we lost touch. I tried to find him recently, called the numbers I have for him, searched the internet, even reached out to his next wife via social media, but got crickets. I hope he's okay.

How did my parents respond? I vividly remember the day I told my mom. I had gone home to Illinois for the holidays, alone, during the time my soon-to-be-ex and I were living in the house together but in separate bedrooms, waiting for it to sell. I went to the grocery store with Mom, and fessed up in the car as we pulled into the parking lot. I remember she would turn on the car for a while to warm it up, then off, then back on several times as we talked. She was amazing.

Mom listened carefully, held my hand, and shared with me that she experienced times when she would look at Dad over the breakfast table and wonder how she could live another year with him. Then she said she would look up after awhile and wonder how she could possibly live another day without him. In hindsight, I suspect that was her way of advising me that all marriages experience ups and downs, and hoping I would try to stick it out longer. At the same time, she was understanding and loving and at least to my face, non-judgmental. She was glad I had sought out counseling for many months trying to work it out, first with my husband, then alone.

The next morning as my dad walked behind me sitting at the dining room table, he squeezed my shoulder. That was his way of loving and supporting me. He never said a word about it that I recall. Ever. I'm convinced he just plain didn't know what to say. I'm also sure he and my mom didn't condone it, but didn't want me to be miserable either.

Many years later, just a couple before he died, I asked Dad how he and Mom stayed married for so long, over sixty years.

He told me, and I think he was serious, "Honey, we just made a pact. Whoever wanted to leave had to take all the kids." With seven kids that certainly would make you think twice.

I stayed single for over twenty years after that difficult divorce experience. Not intentionally, it just worked out that way. I kept picking the wrong men. Not physically abusive men, not really abusive in any way, just them not right for me and me not right for them. I continued to ignore my intuition. One after another would dump me or vice versa, mostly them dumping me. My heart would sting and smart and cry, and I wouldn't date for at least a year, sometimes two or three. This poem pretty much sums up my experiences of heartache in the dating arena during that time of my life.

Sleep or Surrender

Shadows of bruises long past
Whisper loudly through her courage, aghast.
Bewildered by an uncommonly enticing door
She flirts with the treacherous cliff once more.

He appeared just as her heart was timidly freeing
Seductively dancing at the edge of her being.
Quickly her passions were kindled and stoked
Yet her faith and trust remain partially cloaked.

Her resistance may be intuition, too may be fear
Deep into her self and spirit must she peer.
He could be a vile serpent invisibly hissing
Or the peace and ecstasy her soul has been missing.

Like a porch light erases the glittering stars
Her fright may obliterate coming joy, or scars.
Will she sleep through her dreams, dam her heart?
Or surrender to his light, his fire, his art.

But I had a great life that I loved. I had wonderful friends and was riding horses, scuba diving, and traveling for work and pleasure. I was happy. After a while, I would crave having a man to share my life with, feel hopeful, and start dating again. That was when online dating really came into its stride. At first, it was embarrassing to use this service, no one admitted it. And then, after several years, it became the norm. Now as you know it's the go-to resource for many people to meet potential partners.

I met my second husband many years later when I was visiting family and friends in my hometown. He was kind, loving, intelligent, warm, all the good stuff. Again. And again, I ignored the intuitive warnings, and I believe he ignored his own warnings as well. We did love each other for sure, but that doesn't mean we were designed to be ideal marriage partners. Plus, I discovered hand analysis after we had been together a few years, after we were engaged, and shortly before our wedding. Learning hand analysis, diving deeply into the information and revelations in my hands, brought about change and transformation, as it does for most HA students. Subtle and unseen by many but obvious for me.

I've always had a drive for self-improvement and personal growth. I am a different person now than I was even just nine years ago when I got married the second time. Most people may not have noticed the difference, but I sure felt it, and liked it, I might add. But it is difficult on a marriage when one person changes and the other person isn't involved in a similar transformation. Neither track is right or wrong, just different. So we grew apart.

Boy did we try. We went to counseling several times, and I mean several rounds of sessions, not just several sessions. Although it was up and down for a few years, it just wasn't working. We both fought the need to split up for so long. He was such a good man in so many ways, and will always be important to me and hold a special place in my heart.

Not again. I just couldn't believe I was in another unhappy marriage. We decided to part ways the week following Thanksgiving in 2017. It was a brutal time, an extraordinarily difficult discussion, very painful for both of us. Even when divorce is the best course of action for both spouses, it hurts badly. The pain involves failure, loss, and death of a huge piece of yourself. And for me, yet another failed marriage.

Then, during the same week as that horribly difficult decision and discussion, I had to put my horse Comet down. A week I will never forget.

RELEVANT HAND MARKINGS

I have several markers whose Student paths can manifest as challenges with relationships. Two divorces? I guess so.

HERMIT HEART LINE

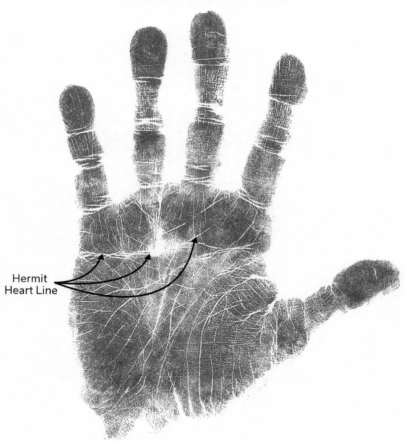

Hermit
Heart Line

One of four possible relationship styles, the Hermit indicates, on the Master path, characteristics of loyalty, integrity, reliability, along with a need for solitary time, space and freedom.

First, I have a Hermit heart line (the heart line represents your relationship style) in both hands. I have a Big Heart too, but the Hermit had the most impact in my marriages. On the Master path, Hermits keep their deepest feelings close in until they trust. They are loyal, need alone time, have high integrity and reliability, and require freedom, lots of it. If others try, consciously or not, subtly or not, to control my time and how I wish to spend it, that will not work. Please be aware this is a different energy than suggesting things to do or asking about an option.

The Hermit relationship style explained so much about me. It explained why, in high school, when boyfriends started becoming possessive or clingy, I would move on. I felt strangled, squished, possessed. I thought something was wrong with me. (Well, there *is* plenty of room for improvement, but you know what I mean.) Other girls would love it when their boyfriends wanted to be with them all the time. Not me. It explained why I never felt lonely, not even as a child. It explained why I don't get it when people, even good friends, flake out. I just don't understand how people could do that. I can't relate.

The primary aspect of the Student path for Hermits looks like trust issues.

MEDICAL STIGMATA GIFT MARKING

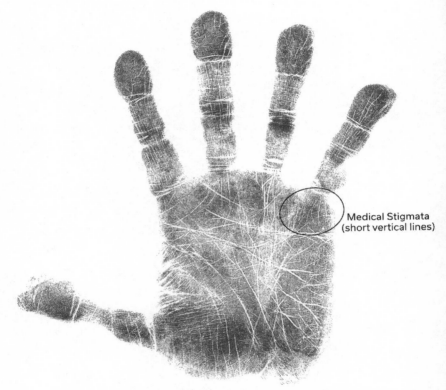

Medical Stigmata
(short vertical lines)

The vertical lines below the pinky finger reveal the most common gift marking, but that doesn't mean it is any less important. This gift provides its owner with hands-on healing capabilities, such as a doctor, nurse, or acupuncturist, and/or an ability to access intuitive psychological insights about people.

I have two gift markings whose Student paths can cause relationship issues. One is the Medical Stigmata, the Gifted Healer or Coach/Counselor. It is one of several markings I have indicating I am meant to help people in deep ways using my intuition and coaching abilities. The Student path? Intimacy issues, starting with myself and then potentially causing dead-end relationships or at the very least, relationship challenges.

MEGA COMPUTER BRAIN GIFT MARKING

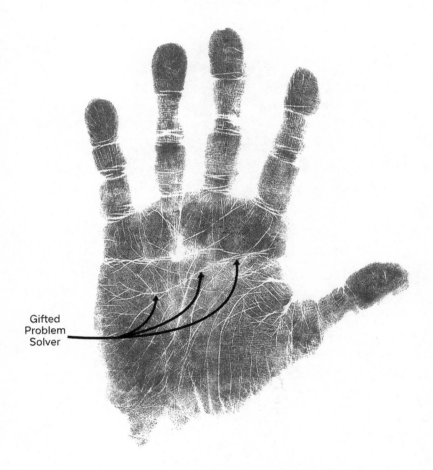

Gifted
Problem
Solver

Often referred to as Hal 9000, named for the computer on the spaceship in the old sci-fi movie 2001 Space Odyssey, this gift marking shows an ability to help people with big issues, big problems.

The second gift that can cause relationship challenges is referred to as the Octopus Brain, Mega-Computer Brain, or Gifted Problem Solver. This gift is half analytical, half intuitive, and very powerful. But when the owner of this gift is not helping people solve big issues, problems that people around the world struggle with, and that make the owner feel important to help with (for me, that means help them live on purpose and love their lives and their work), they will get bored. Then their brain will create problems in their own lives to solve. Fun.

Problems self-created by most people with this gift involve relationships. Relationships comprise the easiest life area within which to create a problem. All you have to do is focus on what's not working, and that attention will make the problem bigger. Well, something is always not working in every relationship.

The wonderful aspect of learning about my markings and their Student paths is the awareness. I've been taking action on these from the day I learned about them. Taking action looks like staying focused on using these gifts, being more open and vulnerable, and working on the self-love aspect of my School of Love. The more I love myself, the more intimacy I can create and offer others. If you don't have an orange, you can't give anyone an orange. Same with intimacy.

How intimate can you be?

Where do you stand with intimacy? What does intimacy mean to you?

Can you be open with your deepest emotions and share them with those people you want to be close to? Can you be vulnerable and accepting of your foibles, your humanity, your endearing lack of perfection, and your feelings?

Vulnerability is the only way to create safety and trust. Relationships without trust and intimacy can be very challenging and often can be doomed.

CHAPTER 7

FINALLY, I FOUND IT

I started a speaking business while in the throes of my Chronic Fatigue Syndrome and Epstein-Barr. I was super broke and had to do something, but going back to nine-to-five work was no longer an option for me physically, mentally, or emotionally. After a few years, my speaking business finally caught on. With Gail's intuitive input, I spoke about gender communication differences in the workplace. I found it fascinating, I knew I would grow personally by learning about it, and it was a hot topic in the late '90s and well into this century. I added a few topics at clients' requests and after several years was doing very well, in the top five percent of professional speakers for revenue. I was traveling a lot, having fun, making a difference.

After about twelve or thirteen years as a professional speaker, the boredom hit again. The not-to-be-denied feeling that I was meant to do something else. Dadgum

it, (That's a southern Illinois term) not again! I was so dis-
heartened. I thought I was on track and had been for well
over a decade. I still had no idea what that 'something else'
was. I thought speaking was the way through to consistent and long-term meaning and fulfillment. Guess not.
Heavy sigh.

The speaking itself wasn't enough, and I was bored
with my topics. As my heart pulled away from the business,
so did the revenue. But I didn't know what else to do, so
I kept doing it. I didn't know how to figure it out. Career
coaches didn't help, and neither did reading all the 'right'
books. I was stuck in a big way. As I watched my speaking
business spiral down, I was faced with the option of hiring
a coach, investing in my business, and hopefully turning it
around. I knew intrinsically I was emotionally and mentally done with that business, and it filled me with dread.
Why would I want to invest a lot of money into something
I didn't want to do anymore? While I was basically poot-
ing around trying to ignore this awareness and hoping for
a miraculous epiphany to drop in my lap, I got hit with
another cosmic two-by-four.

Both my parents died within three months of each
other. Those stories aside for the moment, the V-8 slap of
"Hey! Life . . . is . . . short. Figure it out." hit me like a ton
of bricks. So I started searching online for how to find my
life purpose. I just knew the articulation of my purpose was
what I was missing. After a few months of dead ends, I ran
across a headline for an upcoming teleseminar that read,
"Discover your innate life purpose."

As my breath caught in my throat, I couldn't click that
link fast enough. The first words I read in the description

were "hand analysis." My heart sunk. I was serious here. I really wanted my purpose. I had never heard of hand analysis, figured it was palm reading, and didn't believe that would help me, at least not enough. Then I saw the word "scientific." For the moment, that one word appeased what I call my anal MBA skepticism, so I listened to the teleseminar, delivered by the hand analyst who later became one of my teachers. Surprisingly, it sounded pretty credible.

From the teleseminar, I learned that SHA is not palm reading—no predictions, not dependent on the reader's intuition—but based in the science that the lines in your hands mimic the neural pathways in your brain. And with a database developed over forty years and 30,000 hands. I really wanted my purpose! So I signed up for a Scientific Hand Analysis.

My life changed forever.

It blew my mind. The accuracy floored me. I knew it was right. It explained my whole life—why I had made the decisions I made, why I liked this or didn't like that, why some things worked in my life and why others didn't, why some of my talents and skills came easily and why others took so much effort. I was inspired and on fire from that day forward.

No, it doesn't give you a job description. That would be cuckoo. But I knew the higher-level yet comprehensive and detailed description or concept of my purpose was spot on. I knew it! And I believed if I took action on the Student paths I would be led to the right people to help me, get more clarity, figure things out, and continue to change my life in positive ways. That is exactly what happened, and is still happening.

Within a few months of introspection, finding the right support, and addressing some of my Student paths, the light bulb switched on. Good grief, if I felt so inspired, motivated, and on fire, before I even knew what my purpose looked like as work/career, holy moly this is powerful stuff. I wanted to help other people feel this way. So I decided to learn Scientific Hand Analysis and use it to help people identify their life purpose and live it. I became a Purpose Mentor using SHA as my primary assessment tool.

I absolutely love it. The extremely short version of my purpose is to lead others and help them in deep ways. I have gifts, some of which I have discussed in this book, that I am soul-required to use while doing this work, and doing so helps me fulfill my purpose with joy and make the difference I am meant to make in the world. I enjoyed my speaking business longer than my other careers, and it lasted longer, because I was helping people more deeply than before. But not deeply enough, which is why that career too started fizzling out. The Scientific Hand Analysis made so much sense.

I have referred earlier to some of my markings and gifts that provide the talent, and require me, to help others in deep ways. Several are coaching/counseling gifts. Some are intuitive gifts. Early on in this new career, following many of my coaching sessions, I wondered where the guidance and wisdom came from that would seem to fall out of my mouth. Now I just trust it and know it will be there.

I have the courage to say what needs to be said, most often with the love and connection I have for my clients. I do get emotionally invested with them, and although some critics would say coaches are not supposed to do that, I like that aspect of my coaching style. From all appearances, so do my clients. I fight for them, scare a couple of them sometimes with my passion and commitment, and cry with them as my big heart feels their emotion.

I had always heard that living in alignment with your purpose was important, but so what, yadda yadda yadda. Okay, now I *know* it. Living in alignment with your innate purpose is the *only* way to the deep and more consistent joy and fulfillment that we all crave. And deserve. Knowing you are not on purpose, and not doing enough about it, will kick you in the butt. One cosmic two-by-four after another will come your way—wake-up calls from the Divine, God, Spirit, Source, Universe, whatever you want to call your higher power.

We have a soul requirement to fulfill our purpose. Our souls committed to this agreement to make the difference they wanted to make and experience in this lifetime. If we don't do it, we will receive these cosmic two-by-fours—otherwise known as kicks in the butt, whacks up the side of the head, or life complications. We're not fulfilling what we agreed to do, so God lights a match under our butts. If we don't take action then, He lights another one. And continues to increase the heat until we ask for help and figure it out. Funny how that works. Well, I had certainly had my share of lit matches and two-by-fours. It was finally time for me to step up and out and leave my legacy. I was so inspired.

I took to SHA like a duck to water, and studied it for five straight years. I started conducting hand analyses during the first year, and I'm now a Master Scientific Hand Analyst due to the sheer number I have completed. I got certified to teach this modality, and I am teaching it to others now, others who want to be able to help their clients identify their innate life purpose, special gifts, and blind spots. Others who want to add a very fulfilling revenue stream to their businesses. There are numerous coaches, counselors, and therapists who use hand analysis in their practices. Many of them keep it under the radar for fear of what others will think.

Not me. Once I experienced it I wanted to shout it from the rooftops. And I continue to do just that.

CHAPTER 8

TRAUMA ON THE DOCK

I remember a lot of things about that day. Very little from my childhood before then, though. I remember that it really hurt, physically. It crushed my automatic respect of grown-ups. I remember that I told myself no one could ever know. And I remember feeling sorry for his wife.

It was summer at the lake, my favorite time of year. I was around seven years old, sitting on the dock of our neighbor to the south, fishing with spitballs formed from stale bread. At the lake, we could easily catch and release a dozen or more fish in an hour. It was super fun. This dock was one of my new favorite spots. It sat in the shade of a huge willow tree, and was so quiet. We rarely saw those neighbors, an older couple. Well, older in my seven-year-old mind anyway. They looked like they would be grandma and grandpa to some kids.

I heard a door open and close, and saw the neighbor man Ben walking down to the dock. Cool, I thought, he's going to come talk with me while I'm fishing. Ben sat down next to me on the bench he had built on his dock. I don't recall him saying a word. He put his arm around my shoulders and held me very tightly. I was a little weirded out but nothing major. He was a grown-up, after all, who totally understood them? And kids went to grown-ups for help, right? We were supposed to trust grown-ups.

But then with his other hand, he started fiddling with my waistline, fishing under my shirt to find the waistband of my little shorts. I was shocked, I didn't know what to do or what he was going to do. Suddenly he was sliding his big, gnarly old-man hand down my shorts and underwear. I tried to move away, but he held me firmly. I couldn't budge.

Then he raped me with his hand.

He shoved his big, fat finger up inside me and pushed it around forcefully. It hurt so bad. I tried to squirm away, but he had me held so tightly. Into my mind came my mother's words to never hurt anyone's feelings. I was afraid if I said anything or yelled, I would hurt his feelings, or he might hurt me even more. Very importantly, I didn't want anyone to know what was happening to me. I was mortified, so embarrassed and grossed out. I did not understand it, yuck. He would pull his fingers out then shove them back in for more. My young brain did not get that *at all*. Again, I tried to get away, to at least slide back on the bench a little to lessen the pain. I was trapped. His right arm held me very tightly. And I remember, simultaneously with my shock, feeling sorry for his wife. If she knew what he was doing, her feelings would be so hurt.

Finally, he had had enough and walked back up the uneven brick walk and into his house. Maybe he was worried someone would see him. I was stunned, traumatized. I didn't want to get up and run. I didn't want to bring attention to myself, and I didn't want to show weakness or any clue to what had happened. Funny how my seven-year-old mind tried to cope and repress. Finally, after some time, I have no idea how long, I got up, and tried to nonchalantly adjust my twisted shorts back to their normal position as I slowly walked home.

I told no one until my early thirties. I sought out a therapist at that time only because I knew the experience had to be impacting me in a challenging way somehow. I was so very good at ignoring that.

I remember very little of my life before that event. I always thought it was strange that my siblings had so many more early childhood memories than I did. I didn't connect the two until many years later.

I have worked on this trauma off and on for decades. It certainly impacted my trust of men for many years. I learned way too young how powerful sex and the body can be. Automatically respecting adults or people in authority no longer came naturally to me after this experience. They have to earn it from me. I discovered that secrets eat us up. I decided, mistakenly, that maybe it was safer to shut down, to put a lid on my emotions, my intuition, and all my sensitive aspects.

I minimized and denied the impact of this abuse for decades. Well, it only happened once, I told myself. He didn't 'officially' rape me. He didn't beat me up, I wasn't cut or bruised, at least not that I could see. Many women have experienced much more horrible abuse, so what's the big deal? But it kept haunting me.

It was a HUGE deal. Finally, after being counseled by several therapists, counselors, and spiritual coaches about the depth of my sensitivity, I let the trauma sink in so I could process it.

I've worked through most of the anger, I'm still in some of the grief. Grief about losing much of my young childhood. Grief about the impact this abuse has had on my trust and my relationships. Grief about losing my then-innocent view of the world and the people in it. Forever.

Well, now my secret is out. Oh, I've told many people by now, my mom when I was in my mid-thirties. She didn't let me see, but I'm sure it broke her heart. Ben was dead by then, and I remember her saying under her breath, "Burn in hell, Ben," as we walked along a tree-lined road at the edge of town for our morning walk together during one of my visits. I've told two of my sisters, many friends, even some of my coaching clients if it felt appropriate, relevant, and helpful for them. But writing it in a book is a whole different deal. Yikes.

RELEVANT HAND MARKINGS

BROKEN LIFE LINE

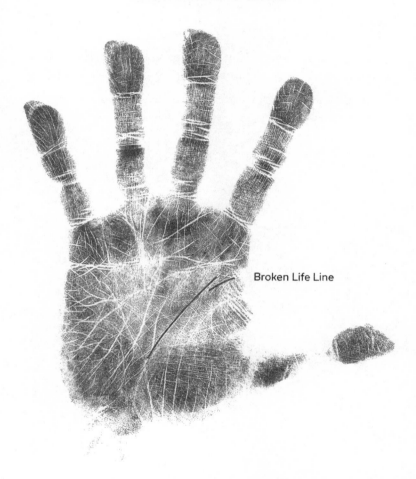

Broken Life Line

One of the possible meanings of a broken or doubled life line is a metaphorical restart, a situation or event that caused a major life interruption.

My sexual abuse by Ben shows up in my hands as well. First of all, my lifeline on my left hand has a break and start-over point, and on my right a diamond near the starting point. Both reveal the possibility of a life-changing event that marked my hands. The break indicates a metaphorical life start-over or huge hiccup, and the diamond represents frozen energy. My early memories were frozen and erased, along with my trust in grown-ups and authority figures. Perhaps also my ability to create true intimacy for several decades. It was certainly an event that deeply impacted my life.

BITTER PILL

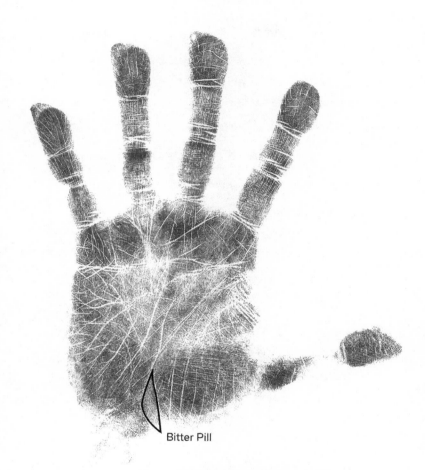

Bitter Pill

This football-shaped marking at the base of the hand can be a little deal or a great big deal. Either way, if you have one, it's an indication of something you certainly didn't like when young.

I also have a Bitter Pill marking in both hands—nice, big, juicy ones—the football-shaped marking at the base of each hand in the center. Bitter Pills are indications of expectations that are put on you when young, something difficult or undesirable to deal with or accept. This could be anything from your parents hoping you would be a lawyer and you didn't want that, to me being raised Catholic when it didn't suit me, or being raised strictly when I have several markers that indicate a deep need for freedom. In extreme cases, this marking can be an indication of abuse or trauma.

How was your childhood?

How about you? Any major childhood challenges or changes? Do they show up in your hands as a broken lifeline or a Bitter Pill? Did you experience a difficult change or event, or feel like you couldn't live your own life, like you had to follow your family's script written for you?

If you experienced trauma or abuse when young, have you gotten professional help to guide you through its processing and release? As most of you reading this book will know, many healing practices, and modalities exist that go far beyond talk therapy. I have used several to my benefit for good mental, emotional, and spiritual health.

CHAPTER 9

TRUE LOVE, WRONG LOVE

I fell deeply in love, the real thing, for the first time at eighteen. I had enjoyed serious boyfriends in high school when I felt I was in love, but the experience at eighteen was unparalleled. I was attending the local junior college because I didn't know what major to pursue so why waste money for university? I never could figure out what I wanted to be when I grew up. I met Nick in class at the junior college. Instant attraction. We quickly became an item, and I was smitten. Nick was fun, passionate, a local baseball star, a good young man. The following summer he proposed, and I giddily accepted.

I suspect my parents were horrified, although they didn't say. I imagine they were praying and hoping in every cell of their beings that we wouldn't make it. Their lack of enthusiasm was unspoken but made it loud and clear that they weren't on board. I didn't ask and I didn't want to know. In my mind, I was old enough to know what I wanted.

Later that summer, his parents invited me to join them on vacation. They planned to drive from Illinois to California and back. I wanted to go so badly. When would I ever get the chance to see California again? (Little did I know that four years later, I would end up living there for thirty years.) My mom reminded me gently that I needed to have a job, but if the bank where I worked as a teller would give me the two weeks off, I could go. Yahoo.

The bank wouldn't. To go on this amazing trip, I would have to quit and hope to get another job as soon as I returned. I knew I could make it happen, not to mention I was headstrong and *really* wanted to go on this trip to the West Coast with my fiancé. So I quit the bank. The day before we hit the road, I got a call from a high school acquaintance—we had worked on the school newspaper staff together. She was quitting her job as a cub reporter at our hometown newspaper and wanted to know if I wanted her job. It would start in two weeks. Holy moly. Done.

On the trip, I got to see much of the western United States, and spend lots of time with Nick. And, I got to see my likely future. His parents bickered and fought the whole way. Nick and I fought a lot too throughout our relationship. It was not my style and new for me, but making up was so heady and passionate, I ignored my intuition about it. I realized on that trip that I didn't want such frequent conflict in a long-term relationship. Also, Nick was excited about the possibility of me working in the post office, having a good pension, and staying in southern Illinois. I knew I couldn't live in his tiny hometown for the rest of my life punching a time card. I came to the conclusion on that trip that I had to end the relationship.

It was heartbreaking. I still loved him. I just realized we probably wouldn't have a happy future together. I mustered up my nerve and gave back his ring. Nick kept calling and trying to see me, but I knew in the depth of my soul that we weren't right. For a few days, my parents didn't know their good fortune. I couldn't talk about it and didn't tell them it was over.

One evening I was in the basement ironing, and my mom came down the stairs. "Honey, your father and I noticed you're not wearing Nick's ring anymore. We can tell it's been very hard on you, and we're so sorry that you're hurting. Would you like to talk about it?"

I could only cry and shake my head no.

Sophomore year started at the junior college that week. Nick and I had signed up for several classes together. I couldn't go, I was both afraid my resolve would weaken and still in deep grief over the breakup. My boss at the paper was a wonderful woman who allowed me to work as many hours as I wanted, so I stopped going to school and just worked. I did not tell my parents.

After a couple of weeks, my boss did tell them, and I totally understood that. The phone rang at my desk one day, I answered, and heard my mom's voice. A huge lump jumped into my throat.

"Honey, you don't have to talk, just listen." She knew I would start crying. "Your father and I know you aren't going to school. And we understand. We know how traumatic this breakup has been for you, and we're so sorry." The love in her voice was palpable.

"There are other options we wanted you to know about. You can wait to go back to school next semester. You can transfer down to SIU (Southern Illinois University at Carbondale) next semester. Or this semester hasn't even started at SIU yet, it starts next week, that's an option too. Whatever you decide, we will support you."

The clear message was that I was going to continue my college education, but that was okay, I wanted that as well and had no intention to stop. That call took place on a Monday. Thursday my dad drove me the hour to Carbondale, registered me for the fall semester, helped me get a job at the Bursar's Office, and on Sunday I moved into the dorm. On with my life.

RELEVANT HAND MARKINGS

SCHOOL OF LOVE

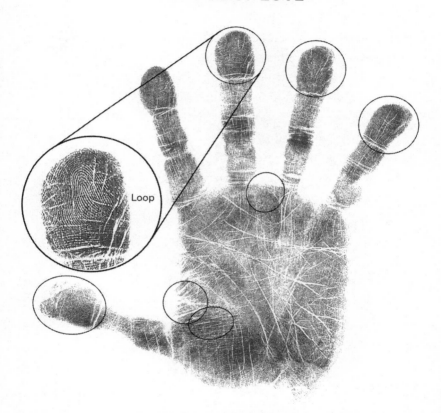

If you have six or more loop fingerprints, you are in the School of Love, the Path of the Heart. Connections, relationships, closeness and intimacy are the hallmarks of this school.

Your school is your operating system of sorts, the overarching energy of your life, the filter through which you experience life and make many decisions. The school identifies some of your natural talents and skills, as well as some of the learning you need to fulfill your purpose. Most people are in one school, many are in two, and some are even in three.

Your school or schools are determined by the types of fingerprints you have. There are four general categories of prints (loops, whorls, arches, tented arches), and each category represents one of the four possible schools. Each school requires a particular number of prints to qualify. I'm in two schools, Service and Love. The other two schools are Peace and Wisdom.

Anyone with six or more loop fingerprints is in the School of Love. Combining my two hands, I have twelve loops (I have several in my palms). Looking at my fingerprints, all but my two index (Jupiter) fingers and my left thumb are loops.

The School of Love is all about connection and relationships, all kinds of relationships—platonic, family, professional, romantic. The motivator for the Student path is fear of losing love. It was my choice, but I lost love big time with that decision, and even though I knew it was right, the pain and grief of that loss were huge for me. The decision, however, was aligned with my Master path as I demonstrated self-love by doing what was best for me, in spite of the loss.

INDEPENDENT THINKER

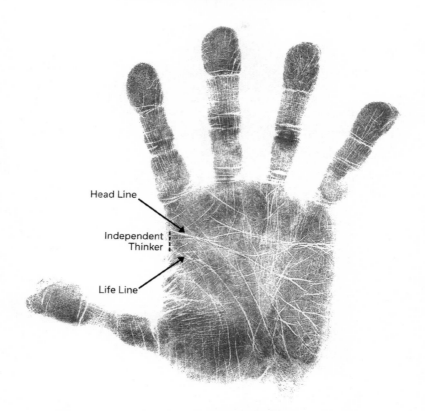

Head Line

Independent
Thinker

Life Line

**See how the head line and life line are not connected at the
origin? This separation reveals independence, that you are
different in some way from your family of origin.**

I have the Independent Thinker marking on both hands.
Approximately thirty to thirty-five percent of people have this.
It shows up as a gap between your head line and your life line.
Both of these major lines originate below the index finger and
above the thumb. The head line usually traverses across the
hand toward the outside edge under the pinky finger, and the

life line curves around the fleshy base of your thumb. For most people, these lines start off connected, then split apart. With Independent Thinkers, these lines are completely separate from the beginning. And mine are particularly wide apart.

Independent Thinkers are more forward-thinking, more progressive thinking, than their family of origin. They often felt different as kids or were told they were different or weird. When older, hopefully, they revel in being a bit of a rebel and out-of-the-box thinker. And, they are independent from their families and crave freedom. The wider the gap, the more independent.

HERMIT HEART LINE

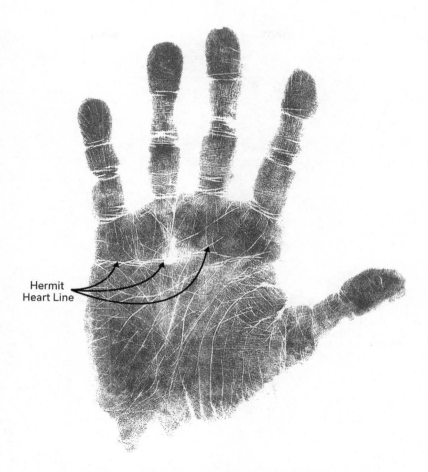

Hermit
Heart Line

Another indication of independence, people with Hermit heart lines need space and freedom. Attempts to control, possess, or cling to a Hermit will not be successful, certainly not in the long run.

A Hermit is one of four possible heart lines, or relationship styles. The Heart line starts under the pinky finger and runs across the hand toward the index finger. Where it ends determines your relationship style or styles. When the line ends under or just beyond the middle finger, as mine does on my left hand, it is a Hermit.

The aspects of Hermit that show up in my engagement breakup story include loyalty, independence, and a great need for freedom. Making a decision that conflicted with being loyal was very difficult. I had to choose loyalty to myself rather than to my fiancé. The conflicts with my need for freedom were the possibility of feeling trapped in a potentially argumentative relationship, limited in a small town (although I ended up moving back there for five years much later in life and very much enjoyed it), and constricted with a nine-to-five job that wouldn't challenge me enough.

Are you in the Path of the Heart?

Do you have six or more loops? Do you resonate with the School of Love characteristics I described? If so, honor your emotions and be authentic to them by expressing them. Make decisions from a place of self-love, not what you think will make others feel loved unless both criteria can be met.

If you have any of the independence/freedom markings, honor that need for yourself. Watch your boundaries and create in your life the freedom you crave.

CHAPTER 10

STORY POTPOURRI

THE SHOVE

She literally shoved me away. The person I loved most in the world. I really didn't know at that young age, under ten, how incredibly sensitive I was. My siblings told me more than once that I was too mushy and sensitive, but I didn't see it that way, it just felt like me.

I had been outside playing with neighborhood kids. I saw Mom through the sliding glass door sitting at the dining room table, reading a book and having a snack. Jackpot. My chance to have some treasured and very rare alone time. With a bunch of kids, at least five by then, alone time with parents was nearly impossible. I ran in and skidded to a stop right by her side, eagerly awaiting my hug. Mom was the best hugger, bar none. Anyone my mom hugged felt completely enveloped in love and rocked gently back and forth as the rest of the world faded away for those

121

treasured seconds. I felt that way until the day she died, and she still has no competitor.

But instead of the hug I craved, she winced, sucked air in between her teeth, and shoved me away. Apparently, in my rush to get my hug, I accidentally stepped on her toe, pretty hard I guess. It hurt and she reacted harshly. "Go on!" she exclaimed as she pushed me away from her, making a mad face.

I was devastated. It sounds so small now but impacted me deeply. I went in for some love from the person I most needed it from and instead got rejection. Do I understand why? Yes now I do, and would have probably reacted the same if someone stomped on my toe. But at the time, and for years, I only felt the hurt.

RELEVANT HAND MARKINGS

SCHOOL OF LOVE

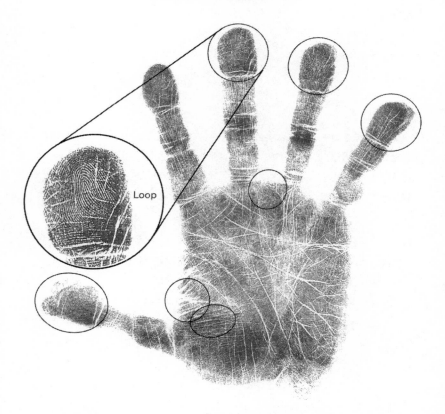

Loop

If you have six or more loop fingerprints, you are in the School of Love, the Path of the Heart. Connections, relationships, closeness and intimacy are the hallmarks of this school.

As discussed in the previous chapter, I am in the School of Love identified by my multiple loop fingerprints. I see it in my life every day. Oh yeah, I'm all about love, connection, and relationships, all kinds of relationships. I love meeting new people and networking. My Hermit has some say in this last situation though. When I'm done networking, I'm done. Often, I see the School of Love Student path aspect that shows up as fear of losing love. Certainly, I'm improving in that area, and some of the stories I tell in this book indicate that. But it will always be there. Remember no one can be on the Master path one hundred percent of the time.

I still stuff my feelings. You saw that in several of the previous stories. I'm working on that too. I still haven't fully processed the grief of losing my parents or my horses. I'm not even sure that is possible.

I don't always speak my truth because I might lose love. I'm still trying to shake the wiring from childhood to never hurt anyone's feelings. Interestingly, because I also have a Ruthless Flip marking, which means I can see the truth and call it bluntly, sometimes I inadvertently hurt others' feelings, but that is not related to School of Love speaking up, really. That School's speaking up issue is more about communicating my authentic feelings about me, the situation, or what I see going on behind the scenes, not so much about someone else unless it is impacting me in a negative way.

Mom shoving me away hurt me deeply in good part because I'm in the School of Love, and felt utterly rejected and unloved. I never mentioned it to her (a missed opportunity to move temporarily from Student to Master path).

Actions to take for School of Love

Many other aspects of my School of Love show up every day, both Master and Student paths. The awareness is so powerful, and will change your life as it has mine, as long as you take action. What action? Speak up when you are upset, angry, or hurt. Try not to interpret people's actions as intentional rejection. Understand that relationships are very important to you and prioritize them accordingly. And especially, live with self-love, intimacy, and vulnerability.

HELPING AND HIP TOO

At sixteen, my dream job was to be a lifeguard. At the time, I was a counter girl at KFC. Lifeguarding it certainly wasn't, but we all (my siblings and I, seven in total by then) knew we had to pay for part of our own college educations, so pushing chicken I did. But lifeguarding really appealed to me. I could help people and be a hip and cool high-schooler at the same time, how perfect was that?

I went to the pool the day they were taking applications. The city preferred eighteen-year-olds. That was my first challenge, but I didn't give up. I begged the city manager, who was there to watch the actual pool tests, to let me try. He was kind but told me I was too young. Persistence came easy for me. I begged more.

"What would it hurt to let me try? Put your biggest guy in there and see if I can save him." He agreed with a bit of a not-so-well-hidden smirk on his face.

My heart sank when I saw who got in the pool for me to pull out. Big guy, a couple years older and more than a little scary to me. Well, I had asked for it, hadn't I? I remembered my Water Safety Instruction training I took a year earlier in the same pool and dove in. I swam toward Steve and dove under just as he lunged for me. I grabbed his legs, quickly swirled him around, climbed up his body to wrap my arms around his chest from behind, and clasped my hands together under his armpit. The battle commenced.

He flipped me around repeatedly and with so much power that my legs flew out of the water and slapped back down every time he rolled. I hung on and waited him out. He was doing all the work, I was just hanging on for the ride and doing my best to snatch some air when my head popped out of the water. I knew he would poop out eventually, or get bored with the determined munchkin glued to his back. And it worked. At least I thought it did. Near breathless, I started towing him toward the side of the pool and, tricky guy, he re-energized and started thrashing again. I held on. Finally, after what seemed like an eternity, I got him to the edge. He climbed out. I was spent. I couldn't get out of the pool and was gasping for air. The city manager walked over, put his hand down, and pulled me up and out of the water. As I sat gasping, he squatted down, pointed his finger in my face, and said, "You, tough little lady, have got yourself a job. Start tomorrow."

RELEVANT HAND MARKINGS

MARS STARS

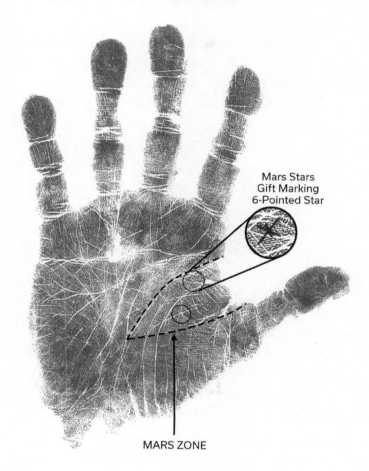

Mars Stars
Gift Marking
6-Pointed Star

MARS ZONE

Six-pointed stars in the Mars zone between the index finger and thumb show up on the Master path as courage, action, and risks.

My Mars markings represent a big portion of my ability to jump into a pool with a huge monster. Apparently, I have guts, physically and mentally. I can be a warrior and very protective of those I care about. I can take action and risks...when I'm on the Master path and can tap into and access my courage, that is. Most definitely, there are things I know I need to do, but I haven't yet been able to muster up the courage to tackle them. No one is on the Master path of any marking all of the time, and I certainly avoid challenges and difficult choices sometimes. Student path behavior can lack courage and show up as not taking the action you know you need to take.

Mars Student path can also show up as anger issues. As kids, my siblings and I weren't allowed to express anger, and rarely witnessed anger to any degree between my parents. So it has taken me decades to dig that out. That said, I've always been an impatient driver just like my mom. I yell at other drivers to let off steam but of course they don't know it.

Decades of personal growth work have reduced this tendency but not eradicated it. Recalling my mom's choice outbursts directed at other drivers always brings a chuckle. At least she was creative in her impatience. If the driver in front of her didn't stomp on the gas pedal immediately when the light turned green, Mom would snap out, "It's not going to get any greener!" or "Pick your shade, pick your shade!" Still cracks me up.

It's rare when I get really angry, which isn't necessarily a good thing. I've learned how therapeutic it can be to scream and cry and beat pillows. The last time I became super angry was after an infrequent but big fight with my second husband. Something triggered me, I don't even remember what, and after he stepped out onto the deck, I threw an empty cardboard box at the sliding glass door he had just closed behind him. I knew it wouldn't hurt or break anything, but my anger scared me. I'm sure it scared him too. At the same time, it felt good to release it rather than stuff it.

BIG THUMB

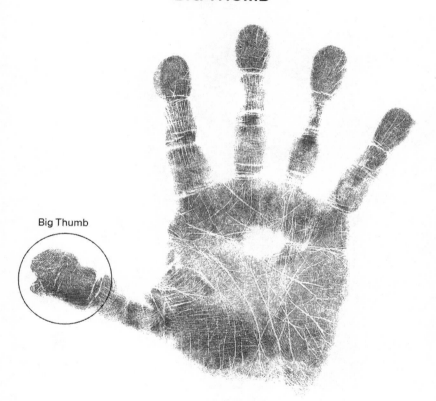

Big Thumb

On the Master path, a big thumb helps you get things done, apply your will and intention, and be persistent.

An indication of my persistence shows up in the top joint of my thumbs. Their large size is indicative of strong intention and willpower. I have the ability, when on the Master path, to set an intention, apply my powerful will, and get things done.

When I'm on the Student path, I have the tendency to apply my intentions for others but not for myself. My strong will and determination helped me get that lifeguard job, for sure.

JUPITER STAR

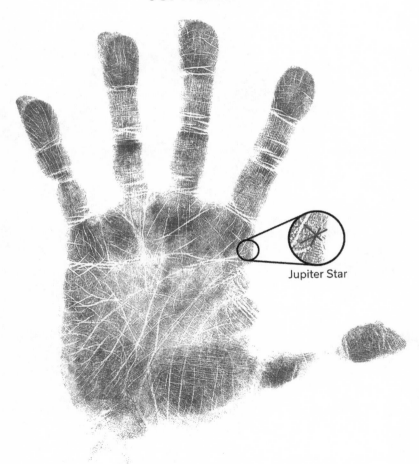

Jupiter Star

If you have a six-pointed star in the mound where your index finger is attached, you can be powerful, influential, a super-achiever, driven, and a natural leader.

In Greek mythology, Jupiter was top god, head honcho, the powerful leader. I have a Jupiter star, which is a gift marking, on my left hand. My Jupiters, the index fingers, are also the foundation of my life purpose so I have multiple Jupiter influences and characteristics. (Purpose is determined by where the highest ranking fingerprints are located. My highest ranking prints happen to be on my index fingers.)

On the Master path of these markings, I am a high-achiever, driven, and influential with natural leadership skills. Quitting or chickening out is not part of being a high-achiever. Do I experience the Student path? Oh yeah. Stepping out of my power, feeling powerless and overwhelmed, hiding out from leadership. I experience it often. But not that day for my lifeguard test.

Do you have a Jupiter Star?

Do you see a six-pointed star at the top of your palm below your index finger, on either hand? If so, then you too have the capacity for great influence, power, drive, ambition, achievement, and natural leadership. Are you using this power, owning and inhabiting it? Have you naturally floated into leadership positions when you were in school, community organizations, or work? Finally, do you resist being told what to do, does that annoy you? If you answer YES to these questions, or at least two of them, you have Jupiter characteristics and may have a Jupiter star gift marking.

IN A SATELLITE SEBRING

I lost my virginity in the back seat of a green Satellite Sebring. I was seventeen and a senior in high school, he was in college. I had been going with Doug for over six months, an eternity in high school. I honestly thought we were going to get married. It was a Saturday night in December, just before the holidays. Two days later, as my mom and I were at the front door saying goodbye to some of her friends, she watched me closely. As soon as she closed the door, she pointed at me and said, "You, young lady, are going to the hospital. Listen to yourself breathe."

I hadn't even noticed. I was wheezing, struggling to get air. The next thing I knew, I was in a hospital room in an oxygen tent with tubes going in, diagnosed with double pneumonia. I was scared and crying, and Mom was right with me, holding my hand under the tent. I couldn't see her. Back then the oxygen was a cloudy white.

The realization hit me that first night in the hospital. *God was punishing me for having sex.* I just knew it in my emotional teenage mind. I was terrified that Mom would find out, or that she already knew. I spent over a week, including New Year's Eve, in the hospital. You would think that might have kept me from doing it again. Nope.

RELEVANT HAND MARKINGS

Certainly, being in the School of Love impacted my decision to have sex with my boyfriend...I was afraid of losing his love if I didn't. My Venus Star had something to say in this story as well.

VENUS STAR

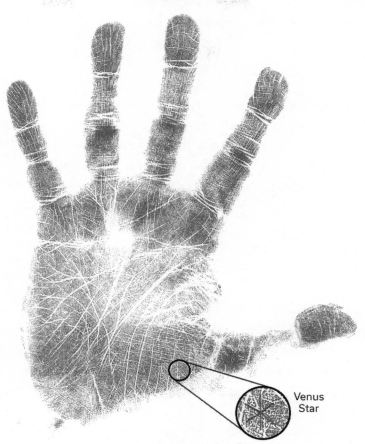

Venus
Star

Venus, the fleshy mound of the hand where the thumb is attached, is the feminine area of the hand. A gift marking here reveals for the owner that fun, pleasure, play, luxury, and delight are important to them.

Another factor involved in this story was my Venus Star gift marking. Venus is the feminine part of the hand, involving personal pleasure, fun, luxury, delight, romance, playfulness, and sensuality. Having both a Star gift marking and a fingerprint (not shown) in this area indicates these feminine pursuits are definitely important to me.

A LIFE TO SAVE

My family spent every summer until my late high school years in a cabin on a lake about twenty miles south of my hometown in southern Illinois. Our fingertips got pruney everyday. We spent hours swimming, fishing, wading to find critters to catch—mudpuppies, frogs, turtles, snakes—all the things kids do on and around a lake. I sloshed through blue-black slimy gooey mud around the edges of coves so much that my toenails would be stained by the end of the summer. I thought that was pretty cool, I loved being a tomboy. Would I do that today? Yuck no.

The neighbors on the north side of our cove had a very mean dog. I'm not exaggerating—this dog was vicious. Queenie, some kind of beagle/hound/lab/pit bull mix, was on a chain and would let you get inside the reach of the chain before rushing out to attack. She was Kujo incarnated even before the movie came out.

Apparently, she let somebody get pretty close, LOL, because she had a litter of puppies that summer. One day I heard loud whining and yipping. I ran out onto our dock to look across the cove and see if I could tell what was wrong. One of Queenie's puppies had fallen off the steep bank onto rocks at the edge of the water, which was lapping over the little guy. He was several feet below the yard where Queenie was chained, and impossible for her to reach. They were both crying and whining.

I had to save that puppy. But I couldn't do so without entering vicious territory. I didn't think of the option to swim over there and get the puppy from the water side. I was fully clothed at the time, and even if I had thought of it, I likely would not have done it because there were water moccasin snakes in those rocks just under the water. I made a decision. It had to be done. I was around eight to ten years old.

I was shaking as I approached her yard. "Queenie, I'm just going to get your puppy for you. Don't bite me, I'm just going to help you." I didn't know I could shake so hard and walk at the same time.

Queenie walked along beside me, growling, snarling, rushing toward me then stopping. I was absolutely terrified, but I kept going. Hearing that tiny puppy crying so loudly, so desperately, motivated me and helped push me ahead through my fear. I kept talking to Queenie, bracing myself for the teeth that would surely rip into my leg at any moment. But it never happened. I reached the edge, jumped down, and grabbed the soaking, cold, little puppy and put him up on the bank close to Queenie.

I earned a new best friend. From that day on, I could go over and sit next to Queenie's doghouse. She would crawl into my lap to take her afternoon nap. I was in heaven. No matter that my mom had forbidden me to go into that yard. I felt so special to be the only one besides her owners that she would allow into her territory.

Overstepping my perceived specialness to Queenie, one day I told my playmate Stevie that he could come into the yard, that if I told Queenie he was my friend that she wouldn't attack him. Wrong. Ah, the naiveté of children.

Queenie patiently waited until Stevie got several yards inside the reach of her chain and then launched like a rocket toward him. He barely made it to safety before the chain jerked her to a stop. Well, in a twisted way that made me feel even more special, but powerless with her at the same time. The specialness won, I was happy.

Queenie's owners gave us one of her puppies, a black male with a white splotch on his chest and white feet we named Licorice. My mom never worried about us playing away from home as long as Licorice was with us. He was one tough dog. He would play roughly too, and sometimes draw blood nipping at our heels when we ran. But if a man approached us out in the field where we played, especially to chase us off the property, well, look out mister.

RELEVANT HAND MARKINGS

MARS STAR AND LOOP

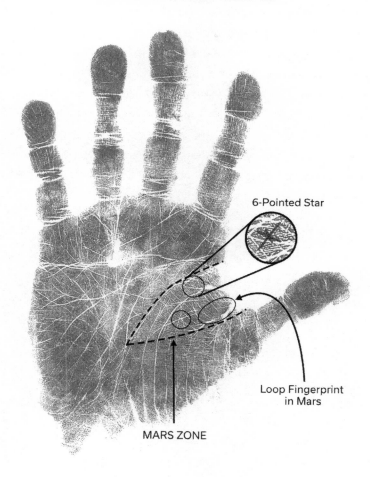

6-Pointed Star

Loop Fingerprint
in Mars

MARS ZONE

Six-pointed stars and/or fingerprints in the Mars zone between the index finger and thumb show up on the Master path as courage, action, and calculated risks.

There is no way to know whether or not I had the Mars Star as a young child because I don't have my handprints from back then to analyze. Most gift markings form after birth as a result of life challenges and experiences. However, I also have a loop fingerprint in the Mars zone, the sideways triangular area above the thumbs and below the index fingers, although it's very difficult to see and doesn't usually show up in prints. Remember, you are born with any fingerprints you are going to have, so I've had this indication of extra potential courage—when on the Master path—since I was in utero. Well, it sure came in handy this day with Queenie.

Do I always take the action I want and need to take? Do I always make the courageous choice? I wish. No one is on the Master path all of the time.

Can you push through your fear?

When has courage called to you and asked you to step up? How did you own it and take action? What did that feel like? Can you see any six-pointed stars or fingerprints in either Mars area of your hands? If so, keep that in mind, and know you have the courage to take action and advocate for the underdog. You will still feel fear, but you have the capacity to push through it and take action anyway.

SHAMAN LOOP

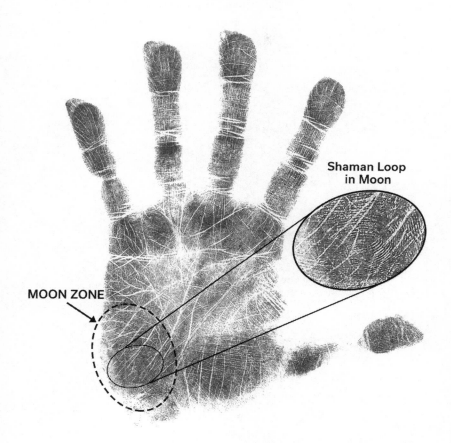

**Shaman Loop
in Moon**

MOON ZONE

This fingerprint, because of it's location deep in the Moon, reveals the owner is not only an intuitive guide meant to help people, but also has a connection to animals, the earth, nature, other dimensions.

This print in my left hand's Moon area indicates a deep connection with nature and animals, along with an ability to help people in deep ways. The Moon area of the hand is indicated in the image above. It is the outer quadrant of the palm at the bottom, below the ring and pinky fingers and across the hand from the thumb. The Moon is about intuition, shamanism, connection to nature, and other dimensions. My fantasy as a kid (okay, I still have it) was to be able to have wild animals feel safe with me and surround me as they did with St. Francis, the patron saint of animals, in drawings on holy cards and in catechism books. I even chose Frances as my Confirmation name for this reason.

NATURAL POWER AND LEADERSHIP

These qualities are as natural to me as my love for horses and dark chocolate. What do people see in me that encourages them to tap me for leadership positions? Confidence, natural influence, decisiveness, the ability for big-picture thinking and attention to details, achievement, advocacy, standing up for my beliefs and opinions even when I know they may not be popular, and certainly, not being easily intimidated. Overall a natural presence and air of authority that encourages people to believe, trust, and follow me.

Shortly after moving back to Southern Illinois in 2009 to spend time with my aging parents, I found myself on two volunteer community boards. In high school, a teacher panel selected me to attend Girls' State, a summer leadership, state government, and citizenship program sponsored by The American Legion and the American Legion Auxiliary for high school juniors. I was deeply honored by this opportunity and vote of confidence from my teachers. At Girls' State, I ran for and won comptroller, in great part due to flurried activity by my campaign manager, my sweet and wonderful new friend Lucy from Central Illinois with webbed toes.

In college, I was voted in as social chairman of my sorority. Yes, I was a natural leader, but I also loved having fun and partying. A little too much back then actually. I remember one specific incident when my roommate and I were sitting on the stairs in our sorority house at about one a.m., trying to remember which one of us just drove her car back from the bars. Yikes.

After moving to Denver, I attended as many networking events as I could to help build my business. I joined several groups and floated into committee positions before I knew what was happening. So many that I had to resign two—I was so overcommitted. I am now on the boards of two high-level business networking groups and a member, with no committee involvement by choice, of three others.

Listing these accomplishments makes me feel somewhat uncomfortable because it sounds very braggadocios to me. (This concern also falls within the Student path of the School of Love—fearing loss of love.) But it feels important to demonstrate how power and leadership can show up in the hands. And, these characteristics are the foundation of my life purpose. They comprise a huge aspect of who I am, and why I need to express my power and leadership to feel joy and fulfillment while making the difference I am meant to make in the world.

RELEVANT HAND MARKINGS

JUPITER STARS AND PURPOSE

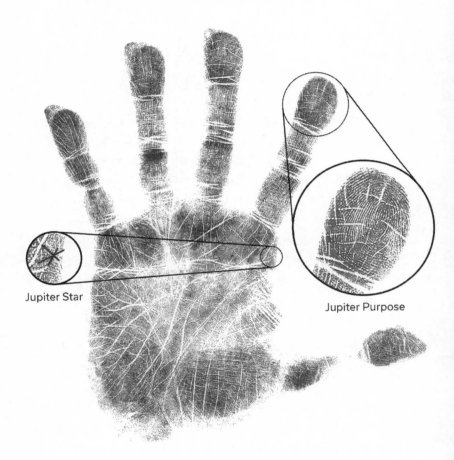

Jupiter Star

Jupiter Purpose

If you have a six-pointed star in the mound where your index finger is attached, you can be powerful, influential, a super-achiever, driven, and a natural leader. The specific type of fingerprints I have on my index fingers make them my highest ranking prints and therefore the location of my life purpose.

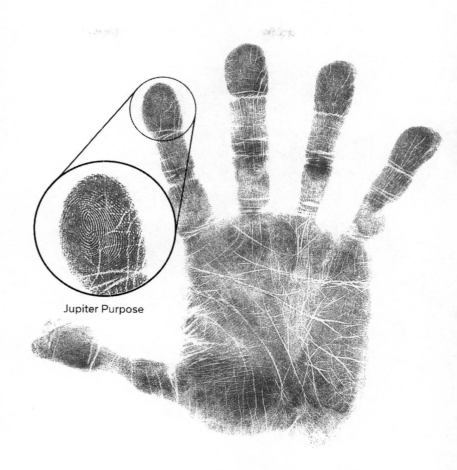

Jupiter Purpose

My index, or Jupiter fingers, contain the foundation of my life purpose. They indicate I am meant to make a difference in the world by being a Visionary Leader and Passionate Advocate. Jupiter is about power, influence, drive, achievement, natural leadership, and the need to create a realm to rule. I have a Jupiter Star as well, pointed out on the image above. This star also reveals natural power and leadership.

Not only have I found myself in leadership positions, but I've created and managed two businesses, also very Jupiter-like.

All that is Master Path. As with all other markings, I experience the Student paths too, more often than I'd like. Primarily, powerlessness and feeling overwhelmed. Giving my power away, not embracing it, working behind the scenes to help someone else get in power. When I am not owning my power, I will often feel overwhelmed. Same goes for anyone else with these markings. And, on the other end of the spectrum, my natural power sometimes intimidates people. Never ever intentionally. But I have several markings, including Jupiter, that make it easy for me to own my power, feel comfortable and confident in my own skin, and call things as I see them. I don't always take the time to think through the softest way to communicate something and therefore can sometimes come across as blunt. Like all my other Student paths, I'm working on it.

CHAPTER 11

TWO MORE

THE FIRST ONE DOWN

Little Lady was the first horse I had to put down. She was at Tanya's ranch, and was the favorite of little kids and stone-cold beginners. Tanya was out of the country on vacation for the holidays and asked me to house- and horse-sit for her. I jumped at the opportunity to live on a ranch and smell horses every day and ride all week long.

Work, of course, got in the way of my daily riding plans, but I still loved it. Little Lady caught the flu before Tanya left, and then colicked. Colic is the leading cause of medical death in horses. Then she got laminitis, which is inflammation of the lamina inside her hoof, an excruciating condition and hard to treat especially in older horses. Laminitis is what eventually killed Barbaro, the famous racehorse that won the Kentucky Derby but shattered his leg two weeks later racing in the Preakness.

Back to Little Lady, her condition eventually caused so much pain she couldn't walk. The farrier's attempts to remedy her feet didn't work. They were too damaged. She stood in the corner in her corral and didn't even move to poop or pee. I was delivering food and water right under her nose and keeping the area under and behind her as clean as I could.

In the middle of the night, during the wee hours of Christmas Eve morning, I awoke with a start. Little Lady was calling to me, telepathically. I couldn't make out any words, I just knew. She was ready to go. She was asking me to help her transition out of her body. After dawn, I called the vet, and then I called Tanya with the sad news and my recommendation. I knew she would trust me, as she did, and communicated how sorry she was that I had to take care of Little Lady's passing. She had clearly experienced this before. I had not and wasn't yet fully aware of how emotionally difficult it would be.

The other women volunteers arrived to find me walking Little Lady up the hill to the area where she would be put down. The vet had given her a nerve block in her feet so I could get her up to where the truck could pick up her body (another awful aspect of losing a horse). We cleaned her all up, more for ourselves because I doubt Little Lady cared that she was a mess. We gave her as many carrots as she wanted, and kissed her good-bye.

She was the first horse I watched crash to the ground. It was traumatic to witness, even knowing her heart stopped before falling. Many months passed before I could tuck that image into the recesses of my mind. It will never altogether leave.

Her Whisper

Through the viscous night her whisper came
Faint but urgent, an undousable flame.
Softly awakening me yet undeniably intent
She asked me for freedom, she gave her consent.

As dark fell to light, her women friends gathered
And brushed clear her soil, to them it mattered.
Carrots and grain tantalized her throat
As needled amber juice set her misery afloat.

She walked once more strong to her passage site
So willing to go, to release her plight.
From all corrals nigh not a sound escaped
Yet equine farewells draped the landscape.

Awash in palpable love from cowgirls near
Her head in my arms, damp with my tears
Little Lady met bliss on Christmas Eve morn
With two closing breaths her soul was reborn.

RELEVANT HAND MARKINGS

NEPTUNE STAR

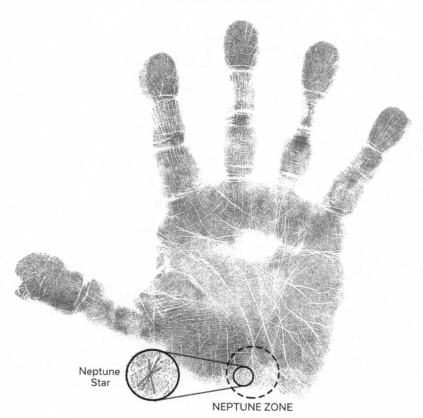

Neptune
Star

NEPTUNE ZONE

Neptune was the god of sea, which represents deep, powerful emotions. Neptune is a small circular area at the bottom center part of the hand, just above the wristline.

At the center of the very bottom of the palm is the Neptune area of the hand, a small circle shape just above the wrist. In mythology, Neptune was the god of the sea, which represents deep roiling emotion. The Neptune Star is an intuitive mark and indicates an ability to help people through difficult emotional transition. It has two nicknames.

'The Empath' is one, meaning an intuitive ability to pick up others' feelings, and also having deep empathy. The other nickname is the Hospice Worker. Neptune Star owners, on the Master path, have the ability to hold space for people in deep emotional transition, including—but not necessarily so—the transition from life to death, without getting wet in their rain. Combined with my Mars markings, I can make the tough decisions, carry them out, and support those transitioning and the people who love them. 'Those' being human or animal.

BIG BO

Bo was another of my favorite horses at Tanya's ranch. He was a huge Percheron, a French draft horse similar to the American Clydesdales. He certainly drew attention out on the trail. He was so big, probably 1,800 pounds, and unusually spooky for a draft horse.

I remember one sunny Friday afternoon, I drove up the long driveway to the ranch, parked, and headed straight to Bo's corral. He was the only horse who had one to himself, not to spoil him, but because he was very aggressive with other horses. With his size, he could do some serious damage, so he got to live alone although he and one of the other horses played together through the pipe corral, which was a good thing. Horses don't like to be alone. They are herd animals, they know there is safety in numbers, so I say 'he got to live alone' with tongue in cheek.

He saw me go into the tack room and come out with his halter, and immediately trotted over to meet me at his gate, nearly shaking the ground with each heavy step. I entered his corral, haltered him, and walked him over to the big, waist-high metal bin filled with a few hundred pounds of grain to scoop up some yummies for him. I was going to then walk him over to the tie-rail and give him the treats. Ummm, that was my plan anyway. Just me raising the lid to the big box freaked him out. Jerking the lead out of my hand, he scrambled over behind a tree faster than I could ever imagine a great big horse scrambling. I turned to look over my shoulder to see where he went, being grateful he didn't trample me during his attempt to escape the metal monster, and saw him behind the tree peeking out around the side.

I had to sit down in the dirt, I was laughing so hard. Picture this—the tree was less than one foot in diameter, and Bo's chest had to be at least two and a half feet wide. It was like me trying to hide behind a two-by-four. Yes, I was very thankful no one got run over, he didn't get hurt, and he didn't knock down the tree. But I giggled about that mad dash to safety off and on during the rest of the day.

Bo was always placed last in the riding string, unless I was leading the ride, because he was so slow. When the other horses galloped up the mountain, Bo would fall back and get nervous about being left behind. During one ride, he got so upset he bucked all the way up the hill. My feet came out of both stirrups so I hunkered down low, grabbed mane, and somehow stayed on his back. The good thing about him being a great big heavy horse running uphill? He couldn't get his big butt up high enough in a buck to do any serious damage. When we got to the top, Tanya was grinning ear-to-ear, and said, "Bo should be your horse, Jayne."

One Saturday afternoon a good friend of mine, Carrie, brought another friend of hers over to ride. I took out Bo, and Carrie and her friend rode two horses boarded with Tanya known for being dependable and easy for beginners. Sharon was all dressed up in English riding gear, and Carrie put her saddle on Salty, a red roan with a very calm disposition. I had never seen Sharon ride, but I had enough experience to know that all the talk and gear and tall boots do not necessarily a good rider make. She may have been, but I didn't know, and I felt responsible for her safety.

Sharon climbed aboard Salty and once settled, her knees were nearly up her nose, her stirrups were so short. I went over to her to adjust them, and she wouldn't let me. "These are perfect," she said.

I responded, "They're really too short for trail riding, Sharon. They may work for jumping but not out here. I really think you'll be more comfortable if you let me drop them a couple inches."

She wouldn't have it. It wasn't an official ranch-sanctioned ride, so I let Carrie know her friend's stirrups were too short, she shrugged her shoulders, and off we went.

The ranch was about a quarter mile from the trail, and all went well till a few hundred yards into the canyon. I was leading the ride, and suddenly heard an unidentifiable commotion behind me. I couldn't tell what it was, I just knew it wasn't good. I stopped Bo, looked back, and saw

Sharon sitting on the ground. No one had ever fallen off Salty. I just couldn't wrap my head around the fact that she came off that easy-to-ride horse. I jumped off Bo and ran back, helped her get back on Salty, and asked once more if she would let me lower her stirrups. Nope.

Salty was freaking out. Not because of the stirrups—I really don't know what was going on. Sharon must have been driving him nuts somehow. I wondered later if there could have been something under the saddle poking him painfully, I didn't tack him up so I had no idea. He kept trying to pass Bo and me on the trail to run back to the ranch. Thank god, I was in front on a huge horse that was difficult to pass. But that didn't last long enough.

I took the shortest route possible back to the ranch, but before we exited the canyon, Sharon lost complete control of Salty. I was shocked at this calm horse's manic behavior. He got around Bo at a wide spot in the trail and sprinted for the ranch, still over a quarter mile away. I watched in horror as Sharon bounced all over on top of him, stirrups way too short to give her any stability. Salty was at a dead run. About twenty-five yards ahead of me on the trail, Sharon fell off, hit the ground head first, bounced a couple times, and let go of the reins as Salty kept running.

I kicked Bo to speed over to her, jumped off and knelt beside Sharon. She wasn't moving or breathing, and I realized she didn't *let go* of the reins, she had been at minimum knocked unconscious, even with a helmet on, and dropped them. I thought she was dead. My mind racing, my gut lurching, I reached for my phone but remembered we did not get cell service in the canyon. CPR was the next thing that popped into my mind. But before I could calm down enough to attempt that, Sharon suddenly gasped. I cannot describe the relief I felt. The air had been knocked out of her. Phew. She wasn't dead, but still unconscious. Carrie went after Salty, and I jumped back on Bo to go get help.

Now, remember how spooky Bo was. I rode him up the street next to moving cars, mailboxes, and garbage cans, right up to big scary gates guarding the very expensive Malibu homes. I was ringing the buzzers, hollering, trying to find someone to help me. Apparently, Carrie had passed a car on her way to find Salty, and those people called 911 because soon a fire engine and an ambulance were screaming down the road right toward Bo and me on their way to the trail. I turned Bo and headed back toward the canyon, not even thinking about how spooky he was and that it was quite possible he would freak and bolt, leaving me in a similar position as Sharon—on the ground. And from that high up? Ouch.

Bo didn't flinch. He did exactly as I asked, kept trotting along even as the fire engine blared by. Then a helicopter flew in and landed about fifty yards ahead of us. He was still a good boy, unbelievable. I didn't have time to think about his extraordinary behavior and that he wasn't his usual spooky self.

Sharon had regained consciousness by then and refused to get into the ambulance or helicopter. Are you seeing the same stubborn pattern I was seeing here? Carrie had returned Salty and her horse to the ranch and arrived in her car. I wanted to get Bo out of there, help had arrived, so we went on back to the barn.

I told Tanya what had happened. First of all, she couldn't believe Bo didn't spook at the emergency vehicles.

"That shows you the power of intention, Jayne," she said. "You were so intent on your goal to get help, Bo didn't have room to question your leadership." Good to know. I learned a lot from that one comment.

"Tanya what should I have done differently? I feel so responsible. I tried to lengthen her stirrups, I had her behind me on the trail, I thought I did everything right." I was in tears.

Tanya listened quietly. She looked me intently in the eye. "Jayne, there's nothing you can do about obstinacy and gravity." Such a wise and comforting response.

Sharon had sustained a broken wrist and had quite a headache. I asked Carrie to call her and make sure she knew the signs to watch out for indicating a head injury— nausea, increasing headache. Sure enough, her husband had to force her to go to the emergency room later that day. She had blood on the brain and ended up in the hospital for days. I found out later she was an alcoholic, which explained the obstinacy and refusal to get medical attention. She knew she would get busted and have to stop drinking. I felt empathy for her, several of my dear friends are recovered alcoholics, but at the same time anger for putting me in that position, and relief for her small children who she was driving to school and various events every day.

Bo was a sweetheart. I had powerful dreams about that horse. Two, in particular, stay with me. In one dream we were walking along a narrow trail with a wall of rock on one side and burning lava on the other side. People were approaching us from the opposite direction, but there was no room for them to pass. Bo was on the lava side. Instead of dropping back behind me to let the people get by, he dropped into the lava because he refused to leave my side. I fell immediately into despair, but I had to keep walking so as not to impede other people. But as soon as the other people passed by us, Bo popped back out of the lava and was beside me once again.

In another dream, he told me he wanted to ride in my car with me and see where I went. He was curious. I told him he couldn't fit, that not even a normal horse could fit. When I got into my car to leave, POP. There he was all squished up beside me in the passenger seat. Somehow, he made himself fit. I ran my errands as he waited for me in my car, then took him back to the ranch, and he somehow popped out and went back into his corral.

A couple of years later, Tanya sold Bo to a children's camp about two hours away. He just wasn't trail horse material, he couldn't keep up with the other horses when they galloped up the mountain, and she couldn't afford to keep him in his own corral. She needed the space for several horses. I hated that, I was devastated, but I understood her dilemma.

About three years later, I drove down to that camp to visit Bo. Three years, wow, I wasn't sure he would even remember me. By then he had turned white from his pretty mottled gray color, which is normal for dappled horses. I hardly recognized him. I grabbed his halter, opened his gate so he could go out into the turnout area, and walked up to him. He was friendly, but I could tell he didn't know me right away. I put my arms around his huge neck, and he buried his nose in my neck and took a big sniff. There he was. Nickering, he horse-hugged me back with his huge neck and nearly stepped on me, trying to get as close to me as he could. I had brought one of his favorite little snacks, a crunchy honey and oats granola bar. I gave it to him, watching my great, big equine love with tears in my eyes. It was super hard to put him back in his corral and leave, watching him watching me as I walked away. I never went back. If still alive, which is very possible, Bo would be in his mid-twenties now.

Heart of No Pretense

His gentleness dwarfed by deceptive disguise
He, his soul, every cell breathes grandiose size.
High massive shoulders anchor head immense
While cradling between them heart of no pretense.

Feathery white lashes cling aloft big brown orbs
Vigilantly surveilling territory unexplored.
A signature snortle confesses his fear
An endearing timbre I helplessly revere.

Mammoth is his love, loyal and sublime
Into enlightened reflection, he accompanied my climb.
Blossoming unguarded, my spirit bestows
Infinite devotion for my majestic, enchanting Bo.

RELEVANT HAND MARKINGS

LOOP IN SHAMAN ZONE OF MOON

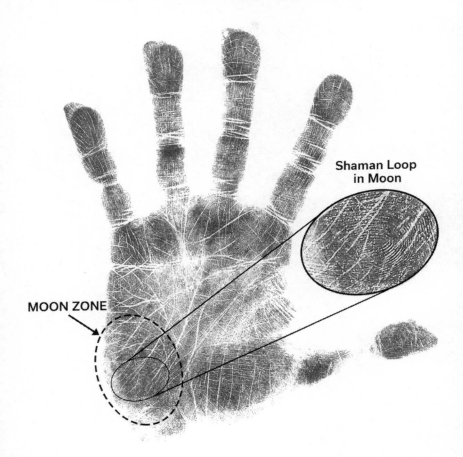

Shaman Loop in Moon

MOON ZONE

This fingerprint, because of its location deep in the Moon, reveals the owner is not only a crisis of meaning expert meant to help people, but also has a connection to animals, the earth, nature, other dimensions.

The fingerprint above, near the outer lower corner of my left palm across from my thumb, is in the Shaman zone of the Moon. The Moon area of the hand represents intuition, other dimensions, and core identity. A fingerprint, in my case a Loop, in the Shaman zone indicates that I'm a spiritual teacher and healer meant to help people through crisis of meaning—any change, transition, event, situation that is challenging for them and changes their core identity, however mildly—with deep connections to nature, the earth, and animals. The fact that it opens to the outside edge of my hand adds to this energy because it's rarer. That, along with other intuitive and heart-based markings in my hands, helped me to connect so deeply with Bo and receive the dreams about him.

JUPITER STAR AND PURPOSE

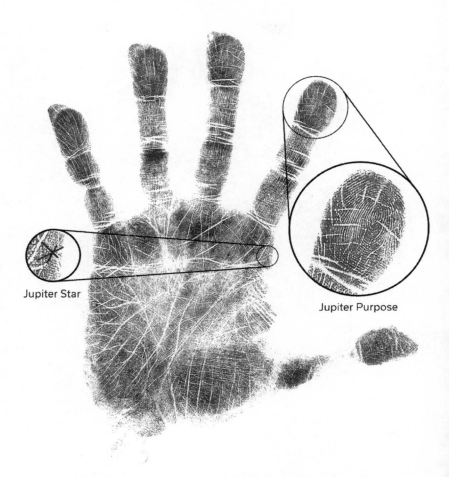

Jupiter Star

Jupiter Purpose

If you have a six-pointed star in the mound where your index finger is attached, you can be powerful, influential, a super-achiever, driven, and a natural leader.

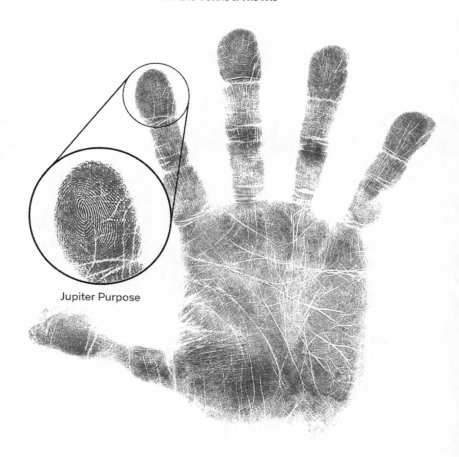

Jupiter Purpose

My index, or Jupiter fingers, contain the foundation of my life purpose. They indicate I am meant to make a difference in the world by being The Visionary Leader and Passionate Advocate. Jupiter is about power, influence, drive, achievement, natural leadership, and the need to create a realm to rule. I have a Jupiter Star as well, pointed out on the image above. This star also reveals natural power and leadership.

Leadership was my primary responsibility at the ranch, both of the rides I led and of the horses I rode. It doesn't always work perfectly, as the Sharon situation demonstrates, but as a leader, I knew at the time and after my talk with Tanya, that I did everything I could short of forcing a sobriety test. Since I had no idea Sharon had been drinking, that was not on my radar.

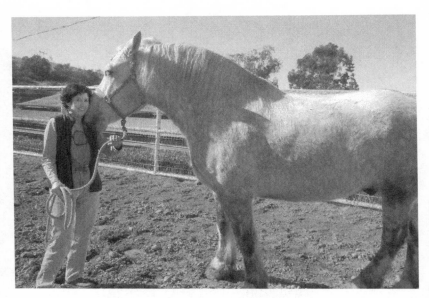

Bo the Percheron

CHAPTER 12

MY BIGGEST REGRET

The summer of 2011, two very yucky things happened involving my parents. Mom was diagnosed with Pulmonary Fibrosis and was put on steroids and oxygen, and Dad suffered a stroke that paralyzed one entire side from the neck down.

I was working at home when my sister-in-law, who lived next door to my parents but was at work at the time, called with great concern in her voice. "Jayne, Jenny (her daughter, my niece) went home for lunch and said MaMary (my mom) was watching paramedics load Pop into an ambulance. Can you get to the hospital?"

I was already halfway out the door before she got to her request. I arrived at the hospital before the ambulance and was waiting for Dad outside the emergency room. He was scared and crying softly when they pulled him out of the ambulance.

"Hi, Dad," I said, and held his hand.

"Hi, Jayne," he responded. I could see he was comforted by having family there.

He never went back home. He went directly to a nursing home where I visited him every day I was in town, either for breakfast or lunch to help him eat. My siblings living in town visited Dad often as well, and even those living in other states traveled home much more frequently so they could spend time with him. Dad continued to decline, the physical therapy did not improve his condition, and when the insurance limit hit, that support stopped. I still visited every day I was in town, and Mom did as well.

One day, I was sitting with Dad in his room when Mom pulled into the parking lot for a visit. We could see her through his window. She was struggling to get out of the car, her oxygen level was so low. She was panting just walking down the hall into Dad's room. Against her wishes I called the doctor, he said to bring her right in (yay for small towns), and I pretty much made Mom go with me. She resisted, I'm sure because she knew the progression of her disease was quite serious. The doctor admitted her to the hospital immediately.

The next day her pulmonologist checked her x-rays, took her off the steroids, put her under hospice care, and told her she had three to thirteen months to live. I wish.

We (the kids living in town) arranged for a hospital bed and brought Mom home to die. The three- to thirteen-month prognosis turned out to be only five weeks.

I think she prayed to go quickly. She didn't want to suffocate, and she didn't want to be a burden to her children. The last week or so she was pretty much comatose. We had her on morphine because her ability to breathe was declining rapidly and causing her to panic. One of my sisters is a nurse and administered all the meds, her care was awesome. Basically, Mom's organs slowly shut down from lack of oxygen.

We each got some time toward the end to talk with her privately. I asked her what she was most proud of about me, what advice she might have, and talked with her about her eulogy. One thing Mom told me she was proud of was the eulogy I gave for one of my high school friends who passed away far too young from ovarian cancer. I asked her if she was okay with me talking at her funeral. She was happy I wanted to, and we talked about the content. I was honored to do this one very important last thing for my mom.

A week or so later, well into Mom's comatose stage, I asked one of my siblings for some input to include in my eulogy. Ouch. Huge ouch.

She told me in a firm and determined tone of voice, "We don't want you to speak at Mom's funeral." It stung so deeply I can't even remember much of anything else she said. I remember something about them not wanting me to say, "Heaven gained another angel." I told her, or at least I thought it, I would never say anything that trite. And I told her I had already discussed it with Mom. That didn't seem to matter. She conceded with a tone that didn't land with me, and with words that didn't even filter up through my awareness at the time, something to the effect of, "Well then don't involve us, make it only about you. And let us read it first."

Sitting on the sofa near Mom's hospital bed, trying to absorb the hurt and shock of what felt at the time to be huge betrayal, I could feel emotion and tears rising quickly and forcefully. As I stood up to leave the room, I heard a soft mumble from Mom.

I leaned over her. "Did you say something, Mom?" She mumbled again but I couldn't make it out. "Mom, can you say it one more time?" I asked. I leaned even closer with my ear right next to her mouth. "I love you," she murmured softly, with her eyes still closed. I wondered if she heard the whole conversation.

I slunk into the bedroom I was staying in and gut-sobbed. I was so very hurt. I was a professional speaker. Mom told me she loved the eulogy I did for my friend. She and I discussed what she wanted. I didn't understand *at all* why my siblings were against me doing this talk. And I didn't know how many or which of my six siblings were involved, had discussed this behind my back, or had stood up for me.

I emailed them all within a day or so to try to gain understanding, but pretty much got crickets. Only one sister tried to explain, but I couldn't see how her input applied to me doing Mom's eulogy. I asked her again about it recently but she truly didn't remember her email or the situation to any helpful degree.

Looking back, I didn't handle it well. I couldn't get out of the hurt. I didn't ask enough questions. Maybe if I had had the presence of mind to go back again to try to get more clarity. Then I realized just recently, there could have been no answer that would have taken the hurt away, that would have made it okay that my own brothers and sisters didn't want me to speak at our mother's funeral.

I can see now that it was likely they were afraid I would misrepresent their feelings, mess it up, be too gushy, or otherwise embarrass them. I couldn't see that back then, but I'm not sure it matters because any reason would have hurt.

I wish I could have pulled my head out of my bleeding heart and done it anyway. I kept telling myself that they lost their mom too, and I shouldn't rock the boat. I totally shoved down my need, my desire, my agreement with Mom to deliver her eulogy. Or at least one of the eulogies, she deserved several and I had no qualms about others, family or friends, doing what they needed to do. I told myself, I don't want to upset my siblings even more, and I sure don't want six emotional people nitpicking my eulogy to edit and 'approve' it. (There's some Jupiter influence for you, not wanting to be told what to do or how to do it.) I decided not to speak.

That decision remains the greatest regret of my life. I am still working on self-forgiveness. I was angry with my siblings for a very long time, and then I faced the fact that only I made the final choice. I could have just written it, gotten up during the service and delivered the eulogy anyway. But I didn't. And because of that choice, I was angry at and disappointed in myself. Now I'm just sad about the whole thing.

Even though traditional but not required for a Catholic funeral back then, no one other than the priest spoke at my mom's service. My mom, who was highly respected in the community, voted Woman of the Year by Business and Professional Women, and ran the hospital gift shop and turned it around to profit. My mom, who was president of the hospital auxiliary, went back to school after my youngest sister was born to get her nursing degree, then eventually became director of home health for our hometown hospital. My mom, who most people loved and adored with some even referring to her as St. Mary. No one from the family spoke at her funeral, no dear friend, only the priest. Good grief. In my opinion, a travesty.

I wrote this for my mom, many years before her death.

Above the Clouds

Like the eagle pushing her young from the nest
She always knew I would be up to the quest.
Even when I couldn't see the talents within me
Her unwavering belief would finally set them free.

About her, wisdom, courage, and love come to mind
Listening, laughing, and quietly cheering aren't far behind.
From her came discipline, strength, intelligence, and soul
Her support and understanding often keep me whole.

She is my friend, my confidante, my biggest fan
For me, health and happiness have been her only plan.
She gave me life, then love, then taught me how to live
From her I learned respect, dignity, the joy to give.

About not having children I have only minor regret
One being, her feelings for me I will never have met.
The other for the unborn child who will never know
Her grandmother's love, its power, and its glow.

She is my rock, my shelter, my calm in the storm
Her insight and knowing inspire me to perform.
She gives me spirit and strength through to my core
With my Mother's love, above the clouds I can soar.

If this happened today, I would have given the eulogy anyway. I would have let the chips fall where they may. I am a different, stronger, more empowered woman than I was before studying hand analysis.

Ironically, one of the bits of advice Mom offered to me on her deathbed was to never forget how important family was to me. I love my siblings deeply. My brothers and sisters are all wonderful people with beautiful families. I helped organize several of our reunions (we haven't had one of those full-family reunions since Mom and Dad died).

For one reunion in 1998, I wrote a poem on the plane on the way there for my two brothers and four sisters expressing my love for them. We were staying at a cabin/tent resort in Tennessee, I arrived a couple days early to hike and enjoy some wonderful quiet time in nature. The kind resort owner not only printed out copies of the poem for me but also gave me keys to go into every one of my family's cabins the night before they arrived to place a copy of the poem on their beds with some homemade cookies that I knew they liked.

Devotion Untamed

While soaring high over the Rockies today
Shivering peaks proudly on display
Once again I am shaken by God's art
Awakening for freedom the depths of my heart.

Bubbling into my chest with a welcome squeeze
Emotions erupt, and any disquiet flees.
For as reunion day nears to my rapt delight
Love for my siblings springs eternally bright.

Simple blood fuels part of the fire's flames
The radiant sites, though, pure devotion untamed.
Bred together, yet diverse as colorful bouquets
I sense their beauty and fragrance from far away.

We forge different rivers and sing distinct songs
Kneeling at different graves, in disparate ways strong.
In body, dispersed carelessly throughout the land
In soul, always joined, inseparable, hand in hand.

For six brothers and sisters my feelings gently rage
Each inspiring a love only they can engage.
I need them to know what my heart has to say
That I cradle them close, forever tight, to stay.

Considering they sometimes told me I was too sensitive and gushy, I wondered at the time if some of them may have gagged down the poem. I didn't care. They were my feelings, and I wanted to express them and let them know how I felt. This was long before my parents died.

My dad died three months after my mom passed away.

I am so blessed to have been in the room with both parents, as or immediately after, they passed. My sister, the same sister who was the messenger of my siblings' wish for me not to speak at the funeral, came and fetched me when she noticed Mom had stopped breathing, around eleven p.m., December 7, 2011, just after I went to bed. I am still very grateful to her for doing that. A few months later, in March of 2012, I slept in Dad's nursing home room his last two nights. I just didn't want him to be alone. Actually, in hindsight, as proud as my dad was, he may have preferred to be alone and not have one of his children there to witness his last breath. But I did what I thought was best at the time, and I was there as he passed in the middle of the night.

I got my love of the outdoors and nature from Dad. His escape was fishing and camping. He was an Eagle Scout troop leader, he'd take his troop camping, and then a few of his daughters to the same place later. I loved every minute of it. We would sleep under the stars, listen to the early morning quail, go fishing, and cook over an open fire. It was fabulous. I still love camping.

I learned at least two of my most beneficial lessons from my dad. For several years, every few months, he would take one of his kids to work with him. Dad was an insurance adjuster and drove all over southern Illinois to do his job. I loved going with him, seeing the countryside, and especially grabbing some rare one-on-one special attention from him.

One day we were out in the country somewhere, on our way to see a farmer who needed an estimate for the repair of damaged equipment. Dad saw him about two fields over from the dirt road we were driving on, and to my little-girl horror, drove right off the road and through the fields as a shortcut.

As we bounced through the tilled rows of dark rich soil, I screeched with alarm, "Dad, what are you doing? You drove off the road!"

He calmly kept on his as-the-bird-flies route over to the farmer, and replied, "Jayne, some rules are made to be broken. It's okay to take a shortcut sometimes. We'll be fine." Good to know. I use this rule-breaking lesson quite often.

A few years later, he was building his own little houseboat to use fishing, mostly for catfish lines at night. He had it propped up on stacks of cement blocks and would climb a step stool to get up to it. One afternoon, I skittered down from one of my favorite 'climbin' trees as we kids called them, and walked over to his building site.

"Dad, how are you going to get the houseboat off the blocks when it's done?" I was very concerned about this apparent impossibility.

"Oh, I'll just cross that bridge when I come to it, honey," he answered, wiping sweat from his brow. He wasn't worried one bit, so neither was I anymore. Lesson number two I use quite often . . . not everything has to be figured out before you start.

Many years later when he died, because no one spoke at my mom's funeral, it didn't seem fair to her for me to speak at my dad's, so I didn't. Neither did I broach the subject with my siblings, I didn't want to add to my hurt. But I was always very proud of him. In one of my communications classes in college, one of my speeches was about my dad, his community service, honesty, leadership, and integrity. Again, no one from the family, only the priest, spoke at his funeral, as well. He was even more involved and well known in the community than my mom was, and a proud decorated WWII Navy veteran. I just can't wrap my head around that.

Hopefully, I'll be able to put this in the past and completely forgive myself. I'm certainly working on it and have made significant progress. But I'm not there yet.

And I so wish, wish wish wish, that I had found SHA before my parents died so I could have taken their handprints. It would have been wonderful to see their purpose and gifts, and learn what I had in common with them.

RELEVANT HAND MARKINGS

LINES OF GENIUS

Lines of Genius

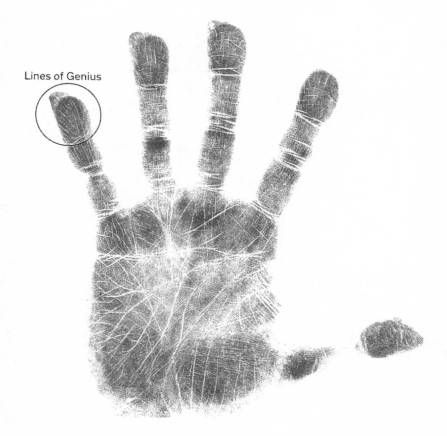

This gift marking, a minimum of three vertical lines in the top section of the pinky finger, from the bottom of the zone at least half-way up, represents an ability to interpret, explain, or transcribe complex or abstract information. It also reveals a need to communicate to groups.

One of the aspects of the *Lines of Genius* gift marking is the need and ability to communicate with groups, writing and speaking. I have shown it here on my left hand, the vertical lines in the top joint of my pinky finger, but I have it on both hands. No surprise I was a professional speaker, it came naturally, and I loved it. Delivering my mom's eulogy would have been for me, a natural expression and aspect of this gift.

NEPTUNE STAR

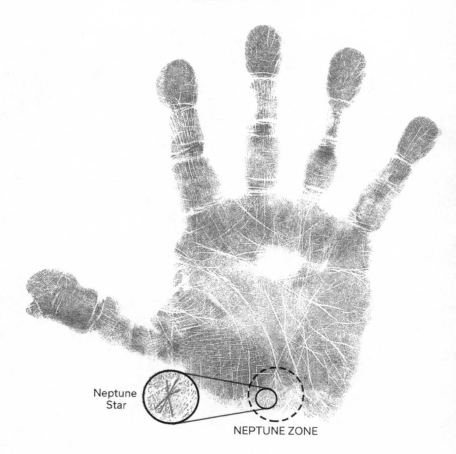

Neptune
Star

NEPTUNE ZONE

Neptune was the god of sea, which represents deep, powerful emotions. Neptune is a small circular area at the bottom center part of the hand, just above the wristline.

A Neptune Star—the six-pointed star at the bottom of my hand in the middle—is all about empathy and the ability to hold space for people through difficult emotional transition, including the transition from life to death but not necessarily so. One of its nicknames is the Hospice Worker.

Until my parents died I had never been with anyone *in the moment* they passed. Horses, dogs, and cats yes, people no. Actually, I had seen only a few deceased people at memorial services, fewer than five. I had no idea how it would feel to be with someone *as* they died. Sitting with my parents during the last stages of life, even as they were comatose and too weak to swallow the saliva in the back of their throats (the accompanying sound is known rather distastefully as the *death rattle*), did not bother me one bit. It was a gift, and I feel blessed and honored to have been able to be with them.

My sister commented late one night, "You know Jayne, not everyone could sit in the room with that noise going on." It was meant as a compliment, and I took it as such.

The Student path of the Neptune Star is being stuck in your own deep sadness, so deep that you need help to get out. Well, that was me in regards to not speaking at my mom's funeral. Profound regret and grief for which I certainly sought out professional support. And most definitely learned from. I can't imagine a future situation where I would stuff down such a huge desire and action already agreed upon by the other person involved.

FAMILY MARKINGS

COMPOSITE WHORL

The s-shaped, yin-yang fingerprint on my left thumb shows that family and community are very important to me, but that my feelings of connection and success in those areas can switch back and forth, off and on.

Oh yeah, I'm certainly different than my family of origin. Two prominent markings in my hands, among others, tell this story. I have a composite whorl on my left thumb, the S-shaped fingerprint pointed out above. The left thumb is about the capacity for success and results (or not) with family and community. The Student path can include feelings of disconnection, not feeling successful with family and/or community, or feeling like an outcast, like you don't fit in.

A composite whorl functions like an off/on switch, and is tied to your Life Lesson. The Life Lesson is your biggest tripping point, your big Kahuna Student path that is your greatest obstacle to living more consistently on purpose. It is everyone's number one thing that keeps them from that more consistent joy and fulfillment. A composite is an uncommon type of fingerprint, thank goodness. And having a composite adds complications because you will experience the Student path more often of the meaning of that location. Here's the deal— when you are in your Life Lesson, which occurs frequently, the switch on a composite fingerprint flips off, throwing you onto the Student path. When you are working your Life Lesson, taking steps to move to its Master path, the switch on your composite flips on, guiding you onto the Master path.

So, since I have a composite on my family connection location, I experience feelings of disconnection more often than if I had a different print there. Wow did this explain a lot to me.

INDEPENDENT THINKER HEAD LINE

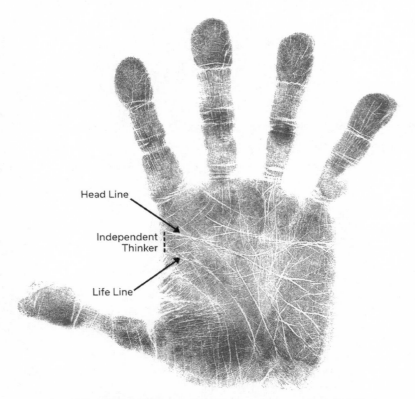

Head Line

Independent
Thinker

Life Line

See how the head line and life line are not connected at the origin? This separation reveals independence, that you are different in some way from your family of origin.

As I've mentioned, I also have an Independent Thinker line. This shows up as your head line not being connected to your life line at its origination point, which is above the thumb. There is a gap between the two lines below the index finger (Jupiter finger) on both my hands. In most people's hands, these two lines are connected as they begin, then split apart.

An Independent Thinker line means I am more forward-thinking than my family of origin, more progressive thinking, more open to different perspectives. It means I may have felt different as a child, or been labeled as such. The difference could be little or big. Did I feel different as a child? I wasn't aware of it until I got older, but as I look back, uh, yes for sure. As I've mentioned, I do remember being teased occasionally by my siblings for being too emotional and gooey. I do remember my mom telling me in junior high that I was different, but I believe she meant it in a positive way.

Another big aspect of being different from my family showed up as not feeling connected to the Catholic church, even as a child. It just didn't make sense to me. Why did I have to talk to a priest who would then talk to God for me? Why couldn't I just confess to God directly? How could it be that innocent babies were banned to a weird place called Limbo just because the adults who were responsible for them didn't get them baptized?

Why was it okay for us to skip church when we were on vacation, but otherwise if we missed Mass it would be a big sin? And was God really that mean, all about punishment and wanting to be idolized? I highly doubted that. It just didn't work for me. Even so, I do feel that particular upbringing made me part of who I am, and I also got a good education in grades first through sixth in our town's parochial school.

As I've grown older, I revel in being different. Is my family metaphysical/spiritual? One of six siblings might dabble a bit, otherwise no, certainly not that I'm aware of. Most are still practicing Catholics, and I'm happy they find value, meaning, and comfort in their beliefs.

How else am I different from my siblings? I'm the only one who decided not to have children. All of them have children, numbering from two to five. It was a difficult decision for me. At first, I felt so selfish and guilty. I grew up assuming I would, but once I realized I had a choice, I needed to give it serious thought. I honestly didn't want my life to change that much, and by that time my first marriage was in trouble as well. I knew having children would not help.

Guess who helped me feel better and more at peace with my decision? My mom. She reminded me that I had a very full and wonderful life and that some people had kids for the wrong reasons. I have never regretted this decision. Thanks Mom.

And once again, the *School of Love*, with all those loop fingerprints I have, comes into play. The primary aspect of the Student path is the fear of losing love. I made the decision not to speak at my mom's funeral in large part because I was afraid of losing my siblings' love.

Are you different than your family?

Do you have an Independent Thinker line? Only about thirty percent or so of people do. How are you different from your family? Do you enjoy being a bit of a rebel and out-of-box thinker as an adult? I sure do. Be aware this marking can also cause communication challenges. We, Independent Thinkers, have a different perspective about things. It's like we're at one end of the room looking west, and everyone else is at the other end looking east toward us, but we think they have the same view as we do. They don't. So misunderstandings can occur unless we ensure others are on the same page with us, or vice versa, after an important discussion or argument.

EPILOGUE

So there you have it. Some of the more emotive stories of my life and how several of my relevant traits show up in my hands. And now, whether you wanted to or not, you know me a lot better than you did before reading this book. You know more about Scientific Hand Analysis, as well.

I hope I've demonstrated the power of self-awareness, at least of the benefits of being open to introspection. I hope I've piqued interest in Scientific Hand Analysis and the breadth and depth of information it holds for people interested in understanding themselves more deeply. And for people open to discovering their innate purpose, gifts, and their challenges so they can take action, make their lives even better, and leave the legacy they are meant to leave in the world.

As a Purpose Mentor and Law of Attraction Coach, I'm devoted to helping people love their lives and their work. I am a breathing, walking example of the contentment that comes from living in alignment with my purpose. My work is so very fulfilling. I frequently offer mini-readings, three minutes long, to audience members when I speak. I have lost count of how many tear up, deeply touched by feeling more seen and understood than ever before. Many women and a few men have choked up during their full hand analysis. I know the feeling.

My clients, numbering over two thousand for Hand Analysis and dozens for coaching, have experienced many life-changing, varied results—going from broke to six figures in under a year, to manifesting a dream job, romantic relationships, much more everyday joy, and inspiring discovery of their creativity. Some have written a book, become sought-after speakers, turned around their misery at work to looking forward to going every day, attracted more ideal clients, and found passion in their lives.

The challenges I have faced, and I'm sure I'll have more (we're never done learning, right?) have shaped me and given me relevant experiences that bring expertise, compassion, and skill for me to guide, support, and help my coaching clients through the transformation they crave.

My ask of you is this—find your purpose and gifts. Figure out the work and life that lights you up and aligns with your gifts and these critical aspects of who you are and how you are meant to make a difference. Take action on your Student paths to help you capture clarity, joy, right action, and the meaning you crave.

Live your purpose and love your life.

Jayne and Darby, October 2018

ABOUT AUTHOR JAYNE SANDERS

Master Scientific Hand Analyst, Purpose Mentor, and Law of Attraction Coach Jayne Sanders helps leaders, business owners, and spiritual seekers love their lives and their work. Her work has been featured in *forbes.com* and other media outlets.

With her unique and profound work, Jayne reveals your innate purpose, special gifts, and blind spots, and then guides you into the inspired meaning, passion, and fulfillment you crave. Her work also benefits corporate leaders, managers, teams, and even children. Jayne has a background in corporate sales and marketing, along with over twenty years of experience as a professional speaker, trainer, facilitator, and coach.

As often as possible, Jayne can be found out on the trail riding her Arabian/Appaloosa horse Darby, or eating dark chocolate. And sometimes both simultaneously.

She has enjoyed such varied experiences as sky-diving from 12,500 feet, bungee-jumping off a bridge over a mountain canyon, laying on the ocean floor gazing at the moon while scuba-diving after midnight, riding the fastest horse in the front of a runaway stampede of over 100 horses and mules, and French-kissing a very large timber wolf that is not a pet. For real. And she watches TV and reads a lot too, honoring her occasional couch-potato cravings.

Darby

WORKING WITH JAYNE

To inquire about Jayne's Scientific Hand Analysis and Purpose Coaching services, learn about her workshops and retreats, buy books in bulk, or schedule her to speak for your group, organization, or book club, please email support@purposewisdom.com.

ACKNOWLEDGMENTS

If I acknowledged every person who made a meaningful difference in my life, well, there wouldn't be room in these pages for my book. Brief words of appreciation do not mean I feel only small amounts of thankfulness.

My love and deep gratitude go to Susie, Talley, Betty, Janet, Nan, Rossie, Lisa, Mom and Dad, Miss Champlain, Bob, Rick, Baeth, Pamelah, another Rick, Rachael Jayne, Judy, Allison, Jordan, Dana, Julie, Tami, Michelle, my brothers and sisters, and all those others I'll think of as soon as the book goes to print.

Relevant to helping me with the creation of this book, a big hearty thank you to Polly Letofsky, Kirsten Jensen, Michelle White, and Jennifer Bisbing.

And finally, for my hand analysis and coaching clients —Every one of you have helped me become a better hand analyst, a better coach, and a better person. I love and greatly appreciate you all.

Made in the USA
Lexington, KY
27 September 2019